# Forgotten Tales of
# Vermont

# Forgotten Tales of
# Vermont

William M. Alexander

Illustrations by Marshall Hudson

THE
History
PRESS

Published by The History Press
Charleston, SC 29403
www.historypress.net

Copyright © 2008 by William M. Alexander
Illustrations by Marshall Hudson
All rights reserved

First published 2008
Second printing 2012

Manufactured in the United States

ISBN 978.1.59629.465.3

Library of Congress Cataloging-in-Publication Data

Alexander, William M. (William Matthew), 1959-
Forgotten tales of Vermont / William M. Alexander.
p. cm.
ISBN 978-1-59629-465-3
1. Vermont--History--Anecdotes. 2. Vermont--Miscellanea. 3.
Folklore--Vermont. I. Title.
F49.6A54 2008
974.3--dc22
2008016756

# INTRODUCTION

Life is ever-changing, and the modern world often eclipses the past. Not too many years ago, the word "Vermont" brought about visions of farms, covered bridges and maple syrup. Much of that has now been overshadowed by liberal politics and other factors of continuing urban encroachment. Formerly, true Vermonters were viewed as hardworking people with integrity, a strong work ethic and independence. Hard work and determination may not have resulted in economic prosperity for many, but their lives were enriched in other ways.

Storytelling and a healthy dose of Green Mountain sarcasm helped entertain families after a hard day of work on the farm. In the days before television, members of a family would gather next to a warm wood stove on a chilly Vermont winter night. Based on activities of the day, local rumors and more, it was easy to spin a tale intriguing enough to hold everyone's attention. Tales of ghostly haunts, unseen monsters and deranged folks were common. It didn't take long before many of these tales became famous (or infamous) legends throughout Vermont.

Scott Wheeler is a native Vermonter who finds and chronicles many events that Vermont history has overlooked. His contributions to this book have been invaluable. I would also like to acknowledge another Vermont author, Joe Citro. Joe is the grand master of all "things that go bump in the night" throughout the hills of Vermont. It was very difficult coming up with or expanding upon tales that Joe has already written about in his many wonderful books. Last but not least, www.vermonter.com is a wealth of historical Vermont legends and was the inspiration for this book.

As a multigenerational, native Vermonter, I decided that writing this book was necessary to help preserve Vermont legends for generations to come. I was born in Burlington, Vermont, and grew up in the fabled Northeast Kingdom, in the city of Newport, Vermont. Although I now reside in Shelburne, I often look to northeastern Vermont as the gold mine best representing the Vermont culture of the past. As you will read in this book, many of the best tales resonate from the Northeast Kingdom.

Within these pages, you will find a variety of strange tales, legends and even a few "truth is stranger than fiction" stories. It's hard to find any tales in Vermont that have been truly forgotten, but hopefully you'll find a few items of interest here that you enjoy. So toss a log into the fireplace, grab a comfy chair and snuggle up with this book on a dark, cool evening. Welcome to old-time Vermont!

# THE STORIES

## THE HAUNTED RAILROAD BRIDGE

During a bitterly frigid winter night in the late 1800s, a fire occurred on the original railroad trestle in Hartford, Vermont. The Montreal Express, a train with passenger cars carrying seventy-eight people, derailed and caught fire. Tragically, thirty-six people were crushed, drowned or burned alive, including a boy and his father. To date, this is Vermont's worst railroad disaster. The old wooden bridge was eventually replaced with a steel structure on the original concrete footings. The bridge spans the White River and Route 14 in West Hartford.

Late at night, people in nearby Hartford often avoid that particular section of road, near the failed trestle. Probably just as well, since the few who have rallied their courage to venture forth have come back in a near state of shock. The lingering scent of burning wood, a ghostly railway worker

and a small boy who materializes just above the river (as if standing on the ice) have been just some of the ghostly events encountered. Touching even the hardest souls are the plaintive cries for help, the wailing and screaming, as if those lost that night are reliving the tragedy over and over again, year after year.

## The "Hubbardton Raid"

Citizens of the town of Hubbardton, Vermont, were up in arms on November 29, 1830, and for good reason. One of their own had been ghoulishly snatched from their midst. Certain of who had done it, three hundred men from town gathered at daybreak. They marched behind the county sheriff on a five-mile journey south to Castleton. Once there, they surrounded the Castleton Medical School building and demanded to be let in. Prying open a wall, they found the headless body of a woman. This, they were certain, was the corpse of one Mrs. Penfield Churchill. The Hubbardton men were shocked and outraged. Although they were thoroughly disgusted, they didn't suspect the Castleton students or faculty of murder. They believed the medical school was harboring people nearly as loathsome as murderers: grave robbers.

The men demanded that the body, and its missing head, be returned. After they agreed not to press charges against anyone for the crime, the dean dispatched a medical student to retrieve it. In their rush to search the building, the Hubbardton men hadn't noticed something earlier. This same student had managed to sneak by the men with something hidden under his coat. Now, he retraced his steps to the haystack in a nearby barn and returned with a bundle containing the woman's decapitated head, which had been removed in a vain effort to disguise the corpse.

The unsavory incident, known as the "Hubbardton Raid," was not unprecedented in early Vermont. Towns near medical schools had reason to fear that their graveyards would be plundered. In those days, it was a not an uncommon occurrence throughout the shadowed hills of Vermont.

The previous section was written by Mark Bushnell and published in the *Vermont Sunday Magazine* of the *Rutland Herald* and *Barre-Montpelier Times Argus* newspapers.

## MAD COW HAUNTING

Between nearby Shoreham and Cornwall, Vermont, a certain angry bovine has haunted a patch of Route 74 since the mid-1950s. A prized Holstein of the Farrington family broke through the fence and wandered out onto the pavement, where she was struck by a local bread-delivery truck. Loaves of bread scattered across the road, and the poor cow was no more, or so the Farringtons thought. Although the farm is no longer operating, a mysterious, lonely cow is occasionally spotted near the same spot where old Farrington lost his wandering bovine. Numerous people driving by the area have seen the white splotches and glowing red eyes of the "Midnight Cow" peering at them in the dark. Some even believe that they have collided with the ghost cow, without any damage whatsoever to their vehicles.

## A LIBRARY STRADDLING TWO COUNTRIES

If you visit the Haskell Free Library and Opera House in Derby Line, Vermont, you may want to have your passport in order. A line on the floor marks the border between the United States on one side and Canada on the other. The cornerstone of the library and opera house was laid in 1901, and the building opened on June 7, 1904. The library's reading room straddles the border between the two countries. There is a rumor that, back in the early seventies, the Beatles had planned to meet at the library. John Lennon wasn't allowed into the United States at the time. Three of the Beatles could have sat on the U.S. side of the line while John could have sat in the same room, just a few inches away, on the Canadian side. Whether or not this rumor is true, the library would certainly be a convenient location for an international meeting of the most unusual kind.

## DORM SPOOKS AT THE UNIVERSITY OF VERMONT

Coolidge Hall, a dormitory, has a few resident ghosts, including a male presence that likes to awaken the residents by staring at them, a playful spirit that enjoys pulling blankets off of beds and a whistling specter that can't carry a tune. The Millis Hall dormitory might have experienced a female ghost on the second floor during the 1997–98 school year. Redstone Hall dormitory residents include a ghost that appears in the back staircase and has been seen running through walls. He's not fond of female students for some reason (possibly pertaining to the circumstances of his death) and has chased frightened students out of the area on occasion. At Simpson Hall, the spirit of a man who stalked a female student to her dorm one year apparently never left. He resides in Simpson to this day. Late at night, students wake up with a sensation of being watched. Usually, the room becomes icy cold when it happens. Some students wake up at night freezing cold and have the feeling that there is someone else in their bed.

## THE FINAL VOYAGE OF THE SS *TICONDEROGA*

The SS *Ticonderoga* started its career in 1906, in the shipyards at Shelburne Harbor on Lake Champlain. For forty-seven years, the steel-hulled side-wheeler cruised the length and breadth of Lake Champlain, carrying passengers, freight and even the automobiles that eventually helped lead to its forced retirement.

By 1950, the aging steamboat was no longer a paying proposition and seemed destined to be broken up for its value as scrap metal. Had it not been for the vigorous action of a citizens' committee, led by Ralph Nading Hill of Burlington, the SS *Ticonderoga* would, today, be just a memory.

Under the efforts of the Burlington Junior Chamber of Commerce and later the Shelburne Museum, the SS *Ticonderoga* (nicknamed the "*Ti*") remained afloat four more years as a tourist vessel. However, the problems of maintaining the aging boat through autumn hurricanes, winter snow and ice; of cleaning, repairing and licensing the ancient boilers; and of finding trained crewmen proved a losing battle. The decision to move the *Ti* to the Shelburne Museum's grounds seemed the best way to avert disaster and to preserve the boat for future generations.

During the winter of 1955, it was hauled two miles from the foot of Shelburne Bay through swamps, across meadows and past a railroad right of way to the museum grounds. The move involved careful planning and unique, painstaking procedures. The SS *Ticonderoga* was floated into a specially dug basin that was filled with water. This would enable the *Ti* to be floated over a railroad carriage. The water was then drained out of the basin, and the *Ti* settled onto its carriage. Tracks were laid in front of the boat, and two months later it arrived at its final destination near the Colchester Lighthouse at the Shelburne Museum.

The journey of such a large vessel overland was without precedent, and the *Ticonderoga* was featured around the world in newspaper and magazine articles and on radio and television. In 1964, it was declared a National Historic Landmark. To move the *Ti* to the museum and provide ongoing maintenance required great and sustained effort, not to mention the commitment of a substantial portion of the museum's annual operating budget. Today, visitors to the Shelburne Museum can walk the decks of the SS *Ticonderoga* in its fully restored glory.

## THE BEE MAN OF MIDDLEBURY

Charles Mraz was an inventive beekeeper who, since the 1930s, had been the country's leading evangelist for the therapeutic use of bee stings. For over sixty years, Charles treated people with bee stings for relief from arthritic pain. Later in life, he treated people with multiple sclerosis and other autoimmune diseases.

Mr. Mraz was widely known among beekeepers for developing a hardy strain of bees well suited to survive in the chilly Champlain Valley in Vermont and for figuring out how to get bees safely out of the way so honey could be harvested more easily.

But many thousands of people with chronic diseases knew him for his campaign to have bee venom and other bee products accepted as medical therapies in the United States—a quest that began when he deliberately bared his own arthritic knees for bee stings. His proselytizing prompted people from all over the world to seek his advice on treatment.

For decades, many sick people made pilgrimages to Middlebury for bee-sting therapy, for which Mr. Mraz never charged. He would pluck bee after bee from a jar, holding each one with forceps as it sank its stinger into the visitor's skin, and then crush the mortally wounded bee.

"Letters mailed to The Bee Man, Middlebury, VT, would make it to his house," said Mitchell Kurker, his son-in-law. Mraz's beekeeping business became one of the largest in New England. At one point, he had one thousand bee colonies, each with a population of thirty thousand to sixty thousand. He ran the business for more than sixty years, until he turned it over to his son William. Today, the honey business thrives as Champlain Valley Apiaries and continues the legacy of the "Bee Man" Charles Mraz.

## BENNINGTON COLLEGE GHOSTS

Formerly a three-story granite mansion, Jennings Hall is now a facility for music students. It was the inspiration for the Shirley Jackson novel *The Haunting of Hill House*. Later on, the book inspired at least a couple of motion pictures. Students and those who work in the building have reported hearing footsteps and voices late at night. Other paranormal activity is also reported, such as instruments that start (and stop) playing by themselves and ghostly voices where no one is present. There have been deaths at Bennington College over the years, and some of the activity is attributed to those who have stayed behind, lingering in the world between life and death.

## THE ORIGIN OF MOUNT MANSFIELD?

From a Stowe newspaper published on August 17, 1858, comes one version of a legend on Mount Mansfield's formation: A giant from the far-off south, many years ago, was walking northward on an exploratory journey when he arrived in the Stowe area. At this point "being fatigued with his journey, as night came on he laid him down to sleep, and unfortunately, he has never since awoke, but like the giant Rip Van Winkle sleeps on." For decades, people have pointed to scenic Mount Mansfield in attempts to creatively distinguish the mountain's "chin, nose and giant forehead."

## A DUAL-PURPOSE COFFIN

Lysander Barnes was a huge man. He towered over six feet in his stockinged feet. "Lys" was something of a carpenter. During the 1850s, he was the "Mr. Fix It" of the north end of Stamford, Vermont.

One day, it suddenly dawned upon Lys that at some time he must depart this life. Realizing that he was of generous stature and knowing the inadequacy of the coffin vendors of the nearby city of North Adams, Massachusetts, he set to work to fix himself a sturdy box of native pine.

His handiwork completed, as the story goes, Lys climbed in to see that the fit was right. He then stored the coffin until the day of need. Now, Lys was a resourceful Vermont Yankee who could not abide seeing things go to waste. The fact that all that smooth, lovely pine storage space was sitting around with no purpose annoyed Lys. So, he decided to utilize the space as a receptacle for beans.

A sawmill and lumberyard were located at the north end of town. Lys sold the beans to the lumbermen and their families, quart by quart. The folks in town laughed but consumed eighty-four cubic feet of beans apparently without any concern about where the beans had been stored.

## THE BLOCKHOUSE

The Blockhouse is the only colonial-era house still standing in the town of Shoreham, Vermont. The house was built prior to 1774, but the exact year is uncertain. It was most likely constructed sometime after 1766 (when the original settlement of Shoreham commenced).

It's referred to as "the Blockhouse" due to its unique construction. On the west side of the building, which faces the lake, thick blocks of wood were placed instead of the regular post-and-beam construction prevalent throughout the rest of the house. This was to keep cannonballs from battleships sailing up Lake Champlain and nearby Fort Ticonderoga from penetrating the house.

Contemporary accounts state that the force led by Ethan Allen and Benedict Arnold camped in this vicinity before the capture of Fort Ticonderoga on May 10, 1775. The men had come along the Crown Point Road from Sudbury, making their way to Hand's Cove on the lake on May 9. They camped in a ravine off of the cove and attacked the fort amphibiously early the next morning.

The party was guided across the lake and into the fort by Nathan Beman, then eighteen years of age. There were seven settlers of Shoreham and two future residents in the attacking band, along with many others from the surrounding area.

The house is on private land near Hand's Cove. Today, it is used as a guesthouse by the people who own the property.

## Employees Who Will Not Leave?

A woolen mill in Barre, Vermont, built in 1842, hosts some nonliving past workers who refuse to punch out and leave. There have been many sightings at the old mill over the past one hundred years. One recent employee worked for almost twelve years and claims to have seen a number of people who haven't quite passed over. She has seen them stitching at the old machines and walking back and forth throughout the building. There have been increasingly strong scents of lilacs present, usually when something supernatural is about to occur. The woman has also seen two different ghosts. When they appear, her adding machine keeps typing the number 3. Other employees have reported similar activity. The building was erected on the site of an old church, which burned down in the early 1800s. Some conjecture that the apparitions could be past parishioners of the church. However, due to the activity, most believe that the spirits are really past millworkers who are still on the job and not ready to leave.

## THE OLDEST LOG CABIN IN THE UNITED STATES

Built circa 1783, the Hyde Log Cabin, located in Grad Isle, Vermont, was one of the first buildings constructed in the area. Built from cedar logs by Jedediah Hyde Jr., an engineer and veteran of the Revolutionary War, it was the home of the Hyde family for over 150 years. The cabin has one large room, heated by a stone fireplace, and a loft above. Many believe this to be the oldest log cabin in the United States. The cabin was moved two miles to this location in 1946, by the Vermont Historical Society, and restored in 1956 and 1985. The Grand Isle Historical Society owns the collection in the building.

## GODDARD COLLEGE'S MUSICAL GHOST

A musical ghost is reputed to occupy the Manor House at Goddard College in Plainfield, Vermont. A prospective student walked into the Manor House, only to find a man playing the piano. The student asked the man for directions, but her question was ignored while the strange man continued to play. She walked out in frustration. She was heading into the upper garden when she turned around and noticed that the piano player was laughing at her. He then vanished into thin air. Similar stories have been reported by others who visit the Manor House.

## UFO ABDUCTION AT BUFF LEDGE

On August 7, 1969, an abduction event took place at the Buff Ledge summer camp for girls on the shores of Lake Champlain, north of Burlington in Vermont. The case was investigated by Walter N. Webb, who spent thirty-two years at the Charles Hayden Planetarium in Boston as senior lecturer, assistant director and manager of operations.

Two teenage camp employees, a sixteen-year-old boy named Michael and a nineteen-year-old girl named Janet, were sitting on a boat dock late in the afternoon. The

camp was mostly deserted as most everyone had left for a swim meet in Burlington. As the sun dropped and the sky darkened, a bright light suddenly appeared. Michael said that he at first thought it was Venus.

As they watched in amazement, the light seemed to grow brighter and to come closer. Then, to their surprise, three smaller lights separated from the larger light and began to perform maneuvers in the darkening sky over Lake Champlain. After a moment, two of the lights receded, but one of them flew straight up and then took a sudden dive into the lake itself.

A few minutes later, the object surfaced and moved toward the two teenagers. Michael later said that he could see two small beings inside. The object moved closer, until it was directly over them. Suddenly, a beam of light shined down from the object. Michael later remembered a floating sensation and then nothing for an indeterminate amount of time. Ultimately, they found themselves sitting on the dock, watching the now-distant light, which flashed an occasional beam until it vanished completely. The UFO may have been seen as it left by three other people returning from the swim meet.

Michael and Janet didn't discuss their experience that summer. Later, Michael would find that Janet didn't remember anything except seeing strange lights in the sky.

Ten years later, plagued by bad dreams, and having read of similar experiences by others, Michael contacted CUFOS (Center for UFO Studies). Walter Webb investigated the case and suggested regression hypnosis.

Under hypnosis, Michael recounted a detailed story of abduction, a medical examination and being taken onboard a "mother ship." After Michael's story of what had occurred was revealed during hypnosis, Janet was located and hypnotized as well. Although she consciously recalled only seeing some lights in the sky, under hypnosis she recounted a similar story of abduction to that which Michael had told.

Webb also conducted an investigation outside the boundaries of regressive hypnosis. He was able to find other members of Buff Ledge who had witnessed strange lights over Lake Champlain on the same night as Michael and Janet's abduction. Two other members of the camp also claimed to have been abducted after seeing strange lights, but earlier in the summer. Their names were not released. The events at Buff Ledge camp are almost certainly proof of an alien abduction.

## Water Witches

Dowsing, also known as "water witching," has taken place in Vermont since the 1700s. In 1799, a stranger named Winchell arrived in Middletown, Vermont. He was wanted for counterfeiting in Orange County and was an infamous con man. He was also a "dowser" who convinced the local populace that he could find hidden treasures and the like. He met another man, named Nathaniel Wood, who had started his own religious cult. Influenced by Winchell, Wood soon incorporated the dowser's "divining rod" into his homegrown religious activities. Wood and his followers became known as "rodsmen" and used their dowsing techniques to look for treasure buried by pirates, to tell fortunes and to predict divine revelation. Winchell also met and encouraged nearby Poultney resident Joseph Smith (founder of the Mormon faith) to take an interest in dowsing.

Although the original interest in dowsing was for such outlandish purposes as seeking buried treasure, it continued on over the years and prompted the change toward divining for underground water sources. In 1960, Vermont became the birthplace of the American Society of Dowsers.

## NOTHING RUNS LIKE A DEERE

Everyone has heard of the name "John Deere," but not many know of its Vermont origin. As the "inventor of the plow that broke the plains," John Deere learned the blacksmith trade in Middlebury, Vermont, as an apprentice in the shop of Captain Benjamin Lawrence from 1821 to 1825. The shop was located below a spot on Mill Street in what is known as "Frog Hollow." In 1836, Deere moved to Grand Detour, Illinois, where, in 1837, he built the world's first steel moldboard plow. Today, John Deere is recognized as one of America's most famous names.

## Where Is Ethan Allen?

In life, Ethan Allen was a controversial Revolutionary War hero whom history often describes as fiercely independent, a bit crude, brash and undoubtedly daring. Allen was no military genius; rather, he was an overbearing, loudmouthed braggart. He was also a staunch Patriot who apparently did not know the meaning of fear. George Washington would write of Allen: "There is an original something about him that commands attention." On May 10, 1775, Ethan Allen, with Benedict Arnold at his side, led the Green Mountain Boys to capture Fort Ticonderoga on the New York side of Lake Champlain.

But where is this legendary figure now? It is known that he died on February 12, 1789, two years before

Vermont was admitted into the Union. What most people believe is that his body rests under the eight-foot statue and the thirty-five-foot granite column at Green Mount Cemetery in Burlington, Vermont. It's very easy to find. The monument is the tallest and most prominent one in the state. The whole structure stands on a solid foundation of marvelous stonework. However, errors in the cemetery records indicate that Allen was actually buried forty feet away from the site first identified as his grave. Archaeologists excavated the area around Allen's grave, based on the cemetery plot map, and found nothing at all. Many theories—from grave robbers to a secret burial elsewhere—are merely guesses. The truth is that nobody really knows for certain where Ethan Allen is buried.

## HOPE CEMETERY—A WORK OF ART

Vermont is home to the "Granite Capital of the World," the Hope Cemetery in Barre. It stands as a magnificent tribute to the stonecutters and artisans peacefully interred among their very own creations. Entering the front gate, you will pass by two granite sentries, forever watchful over their abode. From the moment you arrive, you'll notice that this is no typical resting place for loved ones gone by. It is truly a gallery of splendid artwork in the most unusual of settings.

Since 1895, hobbies of the deceased have been perpetually preserved through ornate stone carvings in the shape of soccer balls, biplanes and even a race car. Perhaps in consideration of the restful living, one monument is a life-sized easy chair with the inscription "Bettini." Another stone is carved in the shape of a bay window. A lady with a bonnet can be seen washing dishes next to a flowerpot through the stone panes. Many other stones depict country scenes of Vermont highways, mountains and forests and beloved homes of the deceased; a tractor-trailer is presumably the last reminder of a man named Galfetti. A tilted cube rests precariously on a stone base marked with "Tree of Life" and the inscription of "Salesman" on the adjacent side.

The truly awe-inspiring statue monuments are perhaps the most ghostly of all. Witness Giuseppe Donati's stone, a bas-relief depiction of a soldier smoking a cigarette, while the face of his wife or girlfriend floats in a wisp of smoke.

## Indian Joe, The Friendly Indian

Joe was born a Wabanaki–Eastern Abenaki. His family name has not been researched, but the Abenaki word for Joseph is "Sozap," sometimes spelled "Suzap." According to historians, he was born about 1739, near Louisburg, Nova Scotia, to a landowning farmer and could have been a descendant of mixed French and Indian heritage.

In 1759, when Robert Rogers attacked the village of St. Francis (Odanak), Sozap/Joseph was probably fighting with the American Indian military for the defense of Quebec and was not present. Soon after this, Joe moved into northern Vermont with Mali, his pseudo-wife. "Mali" soon became "Molly" in the English language. Molly left her husband and family to come to northern Vermont with Joe. This arrangement led to years of pursuit by Molly's husband's family in the hopes of taking her back even though she chose to leave and live with Joe as his wife. They lived and hunted over a wide territory throughout northeastern Vermont—from Lake Memphremagog southwest to the Lamoille River and southeast to Newbury—establishing commercial trapping, hunting and fishing over most of the area and dealing with the local townspeople. The local settlers knew and respected these two Abenakis and often had dealings with them. Joe had warned the towns in and around Greensboro, Danville and Cabot of possible American Indian attacks; in appreciation, they named two ponds in Danville and Cabot where Joe and Molly were said to camp in honor of this piece of local history.

When the Treaty of Paris gave control of Canada to the British in 1763, Joe refused to cross over the border. The story goes that even while following a moose that he had been hunting for a few days, he refused to follow it into British-occupied Canada. At one time when he was living at Hinman Pond, some of Molly's relatives kidnapped her when Joe was away and took her back to Odanak, hoping that Joe would go after her. He refused to follow them into Canada to bring her back; after a few days, when they realized the plan wouldn't work, they allowed her to return.

Joe remained very anti-British, and when the Revolutionary War broke out (1775–83) he was hired as a scout in the Vermont militia. Joe's ability as a scout and guide was highly praised, and he received a letter of commendation and a military pension from George Washington. One of Joe's favorite anecdotes was the telling of the time when he and Molly walked to visit George Washington at his headquarters camp on the North River. He was very proud of the fact that they shook Washington's hand and were invited to sit at the general's table.

When Timothy Hinman's log cabin was built, in the fall of 1794, he and his two eldest children arrived with supplies. Timothy and his wife made many trips between Derby and Greensboro for supplies; on one such winter trip, his wife fell ill, preventing them from returning to Derby and to their children. When they finally could return, they found their children "hearty as bucks and as healthy as savages." They had been cared for by a band of friendly American Indians living nearby in their winter village. More than likely, Joe and Molly were among them. Some stories have Molly being killed about 1792 on an island in the Lamoille River under suspicious circumstances. We do know that Molly died several years before Joe. In 1792, the Vermont legislature passed a Relief Act appointing Timothy Hinman to look to the needs of said Indians.

During the year without a summer, 1816, it is recorded that Joe showed local residents how to find food in the woods after snow and heavy frosts destroyed the crops, making food scarce. Joe grew more enfeebled and returned to Newbury to spend his last years. He died on February 19, 1819, at about the age of seventy-nine. The gun that was found loaded by his side was discharged over his grave. His gravestone reads: "Indian Joe, The Friendly Indian." He is often wrongly referred to in local histories as the last of his race. His birch-bark canoe and his gun are now housed on exhibit in Newbury. Danville and Cabot have Joe and Molly Ponds, and Derby has Timothy Hinman's record books.

## A GRAVE STORY

A walk through an old Vermont cemetery can be a peaceful and even educational experience. It would seem that our forefathers and their early descendants had much more time on their hands than we do now in the modern years. Here is the epitaph written on a stone in Halifax, Vermont, from the 1700s:

*Mr. John Pannel killed by a tree*
*In seventeen hundred and seventy three*
*When his father did come*
*He said Oh My Son*
*Your glass is run*
*Your work is done.*

## GLOWING LIGHTS OVER WAITSFIELD

On June 29, 1977, UFO activity was witnessed from a large open field in the small town. Two fuzzy, glowing orange lights—aligned horizontally about forty-five degrees from the horizon—gradually grew larger and brighter and merged into a single, enormous trapezoid shape at least fifteen to twenty times the size of a full moon. It remained a fuzzy-edged, bright orange light and had no sound. The light gradually shrank and disappeared. About ten to fifteen minutes later, there was just a faint glow in the sky. One of the witnesses said he had never seen or heard of anything like it.

## THE "BOULDERS" OF LAKE WILLOUGHBY

Lake Willoughby is an especially scenic spot nestled between two mountains in the small town of Westmore, Vermont. It is often referred to as the "Lucerne of the United States," and deservedly so. The region has more than its share of legends and stories. In earlier times, Lake Willoughby boasted a fine resort hotel and tourist boats and was host to big bands and tourists from around the world.

Fading ghosts of the past can still be seen as you drive down Route 5A, prompting many visitors to wonder why these old, decaying buildings still remain and what their part in history was. At the south end of Lake Willoughby, nestled among the rocky mountainside, is an abandoned building with a couple of cottages in the rear. A huge rock with the faded inscription "The Boulders" rests nearby, very close to the roadside. The vacant and decaying buildings are a ghostly reminder of days long since past. As you drive past, you can almost hear the phantom music of the dance hall's glory days.

## THE PIPE-SMOKING FISHERWOMAN

During the first thirty years of the twentieth century, fisherwoman Maggie Little was the most photographed person in Newport, Vermont, on Lake Memphremagog. She was most certainly one of Newport's best-known residents. Maggie was born in Bolton, Quebec, on November 12, 1842. Her parents moved to a farm in the United States when she was very young. At barely five feet tall, she didn't have the stamina for farm work. She loved fishing, though, and enjoyed an independent lifestyle. Perhaps for these reasons, she left the farm early to relocate to Newport.

People could say many things about Little, but they surely couldn't call her camera-shy. She was a woman of many hats. She never went to school and was considered a vagrant. Her favorite fishing spot was on the Canadian Pacific Railway bridge. She always wore the same clothes: a long skirt with an apron over it that was perpetually in need of washing. Even though she was constantly near the water, it obviously wasn't to do her laundry or to bathe. And truth be told, fishing is not the passion of a perfumer.

Perched on a barrel, always at the same place, she would fish from morning until night, pipe clamped in her teeth. Folks getting off the train would walk her way to take her picture, as she was only a few hundred feet from the station.

Maggie was a compulsive smoker and would often demand a handout to feed her habit before posing. When she ran out of tobacco, she was even known to split a cord of wood to earn money for more. It seems she was a victim of tobacco addiction; it was her overriding obsession. She sold the fish she caught to feed her habit. If a pipe smoker was around, she would pretend she didn't have any tobacco. Few walked away without giving her a pipeful. Maggie always lived the life of a recluse. She liked to drink beer from a bottle and was fond of the illegal hooch made by W.H. Darling & Son, which legally made soda pop.

Maggie died in 1934, at 91, and could certainly have starred in commercials for the tobacco companies. She did come from long-lived stock, though; her mother predeceased her in 1927, at 103 years old. A lot of water will run under the railway bridge in Newport before there will be the likes of Maggie Little again.

## WHEN THE AMERICAN CIVIL WAR CAME TO VERMONT

Most people (including many Vermonters) aren't aware that the Green Mountain State played a small part in the American Civil War. The St. Albans raid was the northernmost land action of the Civil War, taking place in St. Albans, Vermont, on October 19, 1864.

In this incident, one of the most unusual in American history, Bennett H. Young led Confederate forces. Young had been captured in John Hunt Morgan's 1863 raid in Ohio but escaped to Canada in the fall of that year. Morgan ventured to the south, where he proposed Canada-based raids on the Union as a means of building the Confederate treasury and forcing the Union army to protect its northern border as a diversion. Young was commissioned as a lieutenant and returned to Canada, where he recruited other escaped rebels to participate in the October 19, 1864 raid on St. Albans, Vermont, a small town fifteen miles from the Canadian border.

Young and two others checked into a local hotel on October 10, saying that they had come from St. John's in Canada for a "sporting vacation." Each day, two or three more men arrived. By October 19, there were twenty-one cavalrymen assembled. Just before 3:00 p.m., the group simultaneously staged an armed robbery of the three banks in St. Albans. They announced that they were Confederate soldiers and stole a total of $208,000. As the banks were being robbed, eight or nine of the Confederates held the townspeople prisoner on the village green. One St. Albans resident was killed and another wounded. Young ordered his troops to burn down the town, but the four-ounce bottles of Greek fire they had brought failed to work, and only one shed was destroyed.

The Confederate raiders escaped with the money into Canada, where they were arrested by authorities. A court decided that the soldiers were under military orders and that the officially neutral Canada (then a part of the British Empire) could not extradite them to America. They were freed, but the $88,000 the raiders had on them was returned to Vermont.

## PICKLED POSTMORTEM

University of Vermont medical students who graduated in the 1870s recalled that the school often obtained cadavers from nearby cemeteries. In other states that were less strict about how corpses could be treated, businesses sprang up that sold cadavers. This was particularly true of Southern states, which shipped the bodies of blacks north to medical schools. The practice of shipping bodies had its drawbacks, though. One university student remembered a body arriving from New York packed in brine in a barrel labeled "onions." The person, the students found out later, had died of smallpox. As a precaution, all the students were vaccinated the next day.

It wouldn't be until the turn of the last century that New England states loosened their "anatomical laws." The new regulations helped keep doctors on the right side of the law and the deceased in their graves.

## THE TOUGHEST TOWN IN VERMONT

The *Boston Evening Transcript* headline proclaimed the news on July 29, 1931: "Vermont's Toughest Town Moves to Rid Itself of Gangsters." Prohibition was at its height with two more years to go before its repeal by the Twenty-first Amendment. The newspaper reported that gangsters lolled on Depot Street in Lyndonville, Vermont, parked their rumrunning cars in plain sight and sometimes gave local teenagers high-speed rides on their back-road getaway routes.

## THE SPANISH INFLUENZA EPIDEMIC OF 1918

Nobody enjoys a bad case of the flu, but there are still some Vermonters alive who will tell you that no flu season compares to that of the Spanish influenza epidemic of 1918, an epidemic that killed as many as 40 million people around the world, including about 1,770 Vermonters.

"Today's flu isn't anything like the Influenza of 1918," Nelia Spinelli said, remembering back to the years when tears flowed by the bucketful in her hometown of Barre, as that community, along with other communities around the state, buried its dead. "There is just no comparison. At the time people were dying like flies. It really was a terrible, terrible time. The hearse was going to the cemetery all the time."

The flu hit Vermont in September, at a time when many American soldiers, including some from Vermont, were battling German soldiers in Europe during World War I. Before the flu reached the Green Mountain State, American troops were dying from its effects on the battlefronts. The flu swept into Vermont with a vengeance during the waning days of September. It left as quickly as it came. By the end of October, the epidemic had let go of its grip on Vermont, leaving hundreds dead and changing the lives of countless thousands of others.

## THE MIDDLEBURY MUMMY

This story's origin is in 1883 BC, long before Vermont even existed. That ancient date was when the young son of an Egyptian king named Amun-her-khepeshef passed away and was mummified for all eternity. So what does that have to do with a small town in Vermont? Oddly enough, that is where the young mummy now rests in peace. Rumor is that a local junk dealer named Harry Sheldon purchased the mummy from a New York antiques dealer in the early 1900s. He kept the mummy in his own house, along with a large collection of junk and trinkets (which eventually became a museum of sorts), until he died. After his death, the board of the museum found the mummy and decided it best to bury him in the local graveyard. The mummy was cremated and the ashes finally interred in a burial plot at the West Cemetery in Middlebury, Vermont.

## The Icy Cold Heart of a Vermont Winter Storm

The late winter of 1869 brought about one of the biggest snowstorms in the recorded history of Danville, Vermont. By all accounts, farmers and residents alike would not know just how cold and tragic the storm had actually been until they gathered by wood stoves to read the weekly newspaper. A tragedy had occurred in the neighboring town of Peacham that would embarrass even the most prosperous of its citizens.

The story begins in another town miles away from the Danville-Peacham area; no one is really sure which town. A woman named Mrs. Esther Emmons, seventy-four years of age, had been visiting her son, who had suffered a crippling accident in the Vermont woods. Her son had applied for "assistance" through the town, but local officials were concerned that his mother would also partake in such assistance, and so she was ordered to leave.

Mrs. Emmons said goodbye to her ailing son and attempted to make him feel more comfortable before she set out on foot the following morning with her daughter Mary and her grandson Willie. They were clothed in worn-out, used clothing and carried the few personal items they owned in a small bag. The cold, crisp and clear winter morning stabbed at their bodies like tiny, icy knives. The journey had begun, and they could not go back. Mary was the younger of the two ladies, but Mrs. Emmons set the pace with Willie in tow.

Eventually, they approached Peacham Woods, which could be seen in the distance. The journey was on an uphill route across snow-packed winter roads. Thankfully, the long corridor of tree-lined woods provided some welcome shelter from the harsh winter winds. As they entered the woods, the sun faded away and was quickly replaced by darkening, foreboding clouds—a sure sign of heavy snowfall to come, as every native Vermonter knows.

They trekked another five or six miles before Mrs. Emmons started to give in to exhaustion. It would make no sense to continue on any farther with a storm nipping at their heels, so they decided to find temporary shelter. Houses were few and far between, but they hoped to gain a well-needed night's rest at the first home they came upon. A small house at the foot of the mountain provided a little hope. It was occupied by a man named Bean who turned them away in a less-than-polite manner. Although they were tired, cold and hungry, they would have no choice but to continue onward.

It was midday, and they finally entered Peacham Woods, which meant that the town was nearby. This gave them a bit of relief as they knew their journey was nearly over, if they could just beat the oncoming winter storm. However, they also knew there were still miles to go, which soon dashed their relief. As the snow started to lightly fall, it was both beautiful and ominous. Within minutes, the snow gathered intensity and became heavy to the point that it was difficult to see even a few feet ahead. The snow stung at their faces like needles and piled upon them in a cover of white. Their thin, worn-out clothing soon became covered with cold snow. Each one of them felt chilled to the bone. They hugged one another close in a vain attempt to generate warmth. Their hopes were again raised when they heard the sound of sleigh bells approaching. A man in a one-horse sleigh soon came upon them, and he recognized Mrs. Emmons. He offered to give the old lady a ride into town, but his tired horse could not carry the weight of all of them. Rather than leave Mary and Willie behind, Mrs. Emmons thanked the man and declined the offer. After all, she thought, the next house they came upon would surely offer them shelter for the night. The man flicked the reins and continued on into the storm, quickly vanishing into the snow-filled countryside.

Mrs. Emmons proceeded along, her determination and strength quickly running out. Nearing exhaustion, she exited the woods into open country fields. It was becoming increasingly difficult to walk in the snow. Mary and Willie helped support her while she trudged along, frequently stopping to sit and rest for a while.

The day was nearing its end as what small bit of daylight that remained gave way to the coming darkness. The snow still pounded at them relentlessly, and they were becoming numb with cold. Finally, they reached a farm owned by a man named Stewart. Surely after all they had endured, they had at last found someone with the kindness to extend shelter to them for the night. Despite their harrowing journey and sad appearance—all three frozen from head to toe, in thin clothes and under a frozen blanket of snow—the farmer refused to give them any type of refuge from the storm. He quickly refused their pleas and said he was taking no one in. Turning his back on them, he went back to tending his cattle. Their hearts sank with despair as they slowly continued onward. Not everyone could be so cruel, and surely the next home they came upon would be more gracious and charitable.

The snow was not slowing down, and the darkness of the night was coming fast. Just a short distance farther, the old lady was so exhausted that she had little strength to continue. Her strong will waned with her fatigue, and without her leadership, the other two lacked a sense of direction. Mrs. Emmons fell more frequently, and each time it was more difficult for her to stand up. Eventually, she could only stagger on for a few feet while the others tried their best to drag her along. Hunger, exhaustion and frigid cold were taking their toll on all three of them as their strength dwindled to nothing. The old lady now lay in the snow, unable to summon the strength to carry on. She mumbled incoherently as Mary and Willie stayed by her side for a while, desperately trying to figure out what to do. As darkness overtook them, they decided their only choice was to leave her behind and continue on, searching for help.

Soon, Mary and Willie were lost among the darkness of the night, the never-ending snow stinging at their eyes. They stumbled into a field and noticed a dim light shining in the distance. Tracks visible in the snow the next day indicated that Willie had crawled on hands and knees over a huge snowdrift toward the light that he and Mary had seen in a window. The owners of the house, some 120 feet away, thought they heard cries for help in the night. But with a demented child locked in an upstairs room, they attributed the sounds to her, blew out their lamp and went to bed. Another neighbor living nearby thought he heard one single cry for help but, not hearing a second one, reasoned that perhaps he was mistaken or maybe it could have been the sound of the howling wind.

The snowstorm continued unabated all night long. When morning arrived, the skies were still cloudy, and the temperature was a bone-chilling twenty-four degrees below zero. As the villagers dug out from the snow, a couple men were clearing the drifted road with oxen. A bright piece of cloth was stuck on the sled, a leftover remnant of a bag, perhaps. As the sled continued on clearing the road, they made a gruesome discovery. The sled had been dragging the frozen body of an older lady about half a mile. It was Mrs. Emmons. It wasn't much longer before they came across another frightful scene. The frozen body of Mary was lying face up near a stone wall where she had died without a struggle. Willie's frozen corpse was stiff upright in a snowdrift, where he had turned back to Mary after the dim light disappeared the night before. He was only thirty feet away from a warm fire.

Town authorities soon pieced together what had happened and started inquiries into why such a thing had taken place. Ironically, if Mary and Willie had not strayed from the road they were on, they would have safely reached a welcoming home with shelter. If the Farrows (the owners of the house) had not turned off the light when they did, Willie would not have turned back in confusion and died in his tracks.

The three bodies were brought to the town hall, in the basement of the church, where they were prepared for burial. News of the tragedy spread throughout the community. People wondered how something like this could have possibly happened in their town, which was noted for humanity and compassion. Nearly everyone in town attended the funeral, which was held in the large church where big-box stoves provided the crackling warmth of heat while the wind and sleet were held at bay by the long windows.

As for farmer Stewart, the man who had refused the three people shelter, rumor has it that while on his deathbed, he seemed to be reliving the tragedy. His body shook and he acted as if he were freezing to death. Although it was midsummer when he died, his corpse was as cold as ice.

## BURIED ALIVE IN NEW HAVEN, VERMONT?

Like something straight from an Edgar Allan Poe collection or a book of ghost stories, the plight of Timothy Clark Smith is unusual to say the least. Let's just say that although Tim has been dead for many years, things are definitely looking up…or at least he is.

In 1893, Tim died in Middlebury, Vermont—on Halloween, ironically enough. His body was interred at the Evergreen Cemetery in New Haven, Vermont, in a specially prepared grave. Beneath the odd, grassy mound of earth, Timothy's face was positioned under a cement tube that led to the surface. The six-foot tube ended with a piece of fourteen- by fourteen-inch plate glass, allowing Tim to gaze upward in the event that he was buried alive. A bell was placed in his hand just in case he needed to signal that he was still alive. This brings forth the questions: who could hear a bell under six feet of earth anyway? If he were alive, how long would the oxygen last before someone came to his rescue?

There have been many urban legends of people being accidentally buried alive. Legends include elements such as someone entering into a comatose state only to wake up years later and "die" again a horrible death. Another legend tells of coffins opened to find a corpse with a long beard or corpses with the hands raised and palms turned upward. Fear of being buried alive was elaborated to the extent that those who could afford it would make all sorts of arrangements for the construction of a "safety coffin" to ensure this would be avoided (e.g. glass lids for observation, ropes attached to bells for signaling and breathing pipes for survival until rescued). An urban legend states that the sayings "saved by the bell" and "dead ringer" are both derived from the notion of having a rope attached to a bell outside the coffin, which could alert people that the recently buried person is not yet deceased.

If you want to visit Timothy Clark Smith, take Route 7 to New Haven (a small town just a few miles north of Middlebury, Vermont). When you arrive in town, take Town Hill Road for about a mile or two. Look for Evergreen Cemetery on the left. The grave mound is clearly visible from the road and is about midway between the entrance and exit to the cemetery. Be there with bells on!

## The Curse of Brunswick Springs

*Ripley's Believe It or Not!* called it the "Eighth Wonder of the World" in 1984. To Abenaki American Indians, it is a sacred spot with natural healing powers. Over the last two centuries, people with enterprising ideas have envisioned it as a place of business. Four hotel fires later, they were left to wonder: was it coincidence that led to their failure, or was it the curse of Brunswick Springs?

Brunswick Springs is located well off the main road in Brunswick, Vermont, a town of approximately one hundred residents in the Northeast Kingdom. There are six individual springs at the spot, and each allegedly contains a different mineral—iron, calcium, magnesium, sulfur, bromide and arsenic—that flows into the Connecticut River sixty-five feet below.

The story of the curse begins in 1748, when Abenakis lived near the springs and relied on the natural healing powers of the waters. When a soldier was wounded in the French and Indian War, his Abenaki companions brought him to Brunswick Springs. "Indians said anyone who tried to profit from the springs would fail," says Brendan Whittaker, Brunswick resident and chairman of the town's select board. He says the subsequent fires were caused either by "that curse, someone with a grudge or accidents."

As stories of healing continued to spread, the area began to look like a gold mine at a time when mineral waters were used frequently by the upper classes in Europe. The first house was built on the hill above the springs in 1832. The first hotel, called the Brunswick Spring House, followed in 1860. An early hotel brochure boasts the "medicine waters of the Great Spirit," and "60 guest chambers piped with the water from Brunswick Springs." The hotel stayed in business for several years.

Dr. Rowell, a dentist, owned the hotel, and after he enlarged it in 1894, it burned to the ground. He rebuilt it shortly after the turn of the century and died in 1910. The land was sold to John Hutchins, who took over the hotel, then named Pine Crest Lodge. Three fires in three years soon aroused suspicion. Pine Crest Lodge burned in 1929, and Hutchins had two more hotels built on the land, in 1930 and 1931, before he gave up. Records list combustion of paint fumes in a storage room as the cause of one of the fires, but causes of the other two have never been determined.

Many people who live near the springs still believe there is a strange feeling to the place, as two men hanged themselves in the area, and one woman drove her car into the lake and drowned. A Mrs. Kettle says her brother found a man's body in a tree when he was hunting for partridge in the area, and as a small child, she sneaked down to see it. "It made me sick," she says. "He had hanged himself overlooking the lake."

These days, if you venture to the fabled Brunswick Springs, you will find a wooded area somewhat overgrown with bushes, trees and tall grass. There is a crumbling foundation there, which is all that remains of what may have once been a glorious hotel. The springs are still there and flowing as they have been for many years.

The area is reportedly haunted by American Indian spirits and the ghosts of people involved in tragic events near the springs. Some have reportedly hanged themselves in the quiet, isolated area, and an infant was found strangled to death and abandoned there. In the late 1990s, an infamous murderer was tracked down and killed by police near the haunted Brunswick Springs. Apparently, the curse is still claiming hapless victims.

## The Battle of Bennington?

On the afternoon of August 16, 1777, a Revolutionary War battle took place that resulted in a colonial victory. A force of 2,000 New Hampshire and Massachusetts militiamen—led by General John Stark with aid from

Colonel Seth Warner, along with elements of Vermont's Green Mountain Boys—defeated a combined force of 1,250 dismounted Brunswick dragoons, Canadians, Loyalists and American Indians, led by Lieutenant Colonel Friedrich Baum. To this day, August 16 is celebrated as a legal holiday in Vermont, and a 306-foot-tall Bennington Battle monument commemorates the battle.

The odd thing about this celebrated battle is that it didn't actually take place in Bennington, Vermont, but about ten miles away in Walloomsac, New York.

## THE RESURRECTION MEN

Much of what is known about grave robbing in Vermont comes from Frederick Waite, who taught embryology and histology at Case Western Reserve University in Cleveland. Waite estimated that, based on the number of medical students in Vermont, the state's medical schools (in Burlington, Castleton and Woodstock) would have required at least four hundred cadavers between 1820 and 1840.

In his research, Waite found, not surprisingly, that most grave robberies occurred near the medical schools. Remote cemeteries were the most often hit. A village cemetery was too close to prying eyes. Once someone at the school learned of a nearby funeral, a team of robbers would set to work. First, a scout, disguised as a hunter, was often sent out to locate the grave exactly. The robbers would return at night and need a precise location.

On the night of the robbery, almost invariably the night of the funeral, since bodies were not then embalmed, a team of three men would travel by wagon to the cemetery. The men, often referred to as "resurrection men," were usually laborers hired to do the job, Waite theorizes, since most medical students wouldn't have been up to the physically demanding task.

Two of the men would hop out at the cemetery and carry their tools to the grave. If the cemetery was near a well-traveled road, the third man would drive off, only to return at a set time. A wagon sitting at night by a cemetery would have been a sure tip-off.

Though the men were in a hurry, they were careful. Working by the dim light of a shrouded lantern, they would study the surface of the freshly dug grave for any pattern of sticks or leaves that might have been left there by a friend of the deceased to detect grave robbing. They would map how any such items lay and then set to work.

To speed things up, according to Waite, they would not excavate the entire grave. Instead, they would dig a roughly three-foot by three-foot hole at the head of the grave. All the dirt would be placed on a tarpaulin to avoid letting it fall onto the surrounding grass, another telltale sign of robbery. Once they reached the casket, which was usually down about four feet, they would drill a series of holes into it with an auger, an axe or saw being too noisy for the job.

After part of the casket lid was removed, they would lower a hook connected to a chain and a long metal bar into the grave and place it under the chin of the corpse. Then the two men would haul the body out and place it on a second tarp. They would remove any clothes from the body—which would just have to be disposed of later, anyway—and toss them into the open grave.

Then they would carefully replace the dirt in the grave. Fearing they might leave a tool behind, they would count them as they placed them onto a tarp before lugging the tools and the corpse to the waiting wagon. A competent team could do the job in about an hour.

The odd thing Waite found was that during that period, authorities only issued seven indictments for grave robbing. They involved four separate incidents. If you accept Waite's estimates, nobody was charged in 99 percent of the state's grave robberies. In many cases, the robbers may have been so deft that their crime was never detected. As a result, unbeknownst to most Vermonters, many graves in the state lie empty.

The previous section was written by Mark Bushnell and published in the *Vermont Sunday Magazine* of the *Rutland Herald* and *Barre-Montpelier Times Argus* newspapers.

## LAKE WILLOUGHBY MONSTER AND OTHER ODDITIES

Willoughby Lake is a scenic body of water located in the northern Vermont town of Westmore, nestled between two mountains, Mount Hor and Mount Pisgah. In earlier years, the region was a well-known and popular destination with several large tourist hotels and much to see and do.

On August 14, 1868, the story of a "lake monster" appeared in the Caledonian newspaper. "It is reported that the great water snake at Willoughby Lake was killed Wednesday of last week by Stephen Edmonds of Newport, Vermont, a lad of twelve years. Rushing boldly upon the monster he severed its body with a sickle. On actual measurement the two pieces were found to be 23 feet in length."

Perhaps the "monster" could have been a huge eel. A local resident, P.M. "Bun" Daniels of Westmore, said that eels have been caught near Gilman Tavern, but none of them would have reached anywhere near the proportions reported by young Stephen Edmonds.

According to local folklore, there is an underground passageway between Lake Willoughby and Crystal Lake in the nearby town of Barton. One local legend states that, many years ago, a team of horses crashed through the winter ice on Lake Willoughby only to be found months later during warmer months in Crystal Lake, several miles away.

## A HEADSTONE THAT SAYS IT ALL

If your journeys take you to the town of Pownal, Vermont, you may come across a cemetery that contains a headstone with the following inscription:

> *Here lies as silent clay*
> *Miss Arabella Young*
> *Who on the 21$^{st}$ of May 1771*
> *Began to hold her tongue*

## WORLD WAR II BOMBERS CRASH IN VERMONT

Two U.S. Army Air Corps bombers crashed in Vermont during World War II. On June 27, 1943, a B-17 Flying Fortress bomber en route from Nebraska to Maine crashed into Fish Hill in Randolph, Vermont. Seven of the crew managed to bail out, but three died in the crash.

On October 16, 1944, an Army Air Corps B-24 Liberator bomber on a training mission from Westover Field in Chicopee, Massachusetts, crashed into the side of Camel's Hump mountain in Vermont. The state's worst

aviation disaster of the time killed nine of the ten crewmen onboard. Even to this day, remains of the wreckage are still visible at the site of the crash.

## THE HAYDEN FAMILY CURSE

Legend has it that, many years ago, the entire Hayden family perished as victims of a curse. In 1910, a horse-drawn hearse carried the final remains of William Henry Hayden, last in the male line of his family, along the South Albany Road to the village cemetery. Curtains were drawn across the mansion's windows in tribute, even though the extravagantly furnished house had remained without a tenant for nearly twenty years. Some would remember Mercie Dale's curse on the family that the Hayden family name would die and pass into oblivion. What would happen now to the vacant, dark mansion with its wide fields and impressive barns? Was there a hidden family fortune, and if so, where had it been secreted away? Those answers and other secrets lie within the final resting place of Henry Hayden.

Over the years, William acquired so much land that, in 1823, he found himself in serious financial trouble. His mother-in-law, Mercie Dale, had given him money over the years to help, but it had never been repaid, and he continued to ask for more. Suspicion set in, and Mercie Dale fell victim to a long illness, accusing William of poisoning her.

As the end came, Mercie uttered her ominous curse in the presence of her daughter, Silence: "The Hayden name shall die in the third generation, and the last to bear the name shall die in poverty." In the final days, neighbor Sally Rogers cared for Mercie until she died. Her body was interred in the Rogers family cemetery as Mercie refused to lie within the same cemetery as the Haydens.

Once the new mansion was built, the Haydens enjoyed a privileged life that was the envy of the region. Pleasure rides in the handsome, horse-drawn carriages would often be the order of the day. There were servants to wait on family members. A New Year's Eve grand party would be held on the third-floor ballroom. For the most part, life was going well for the Haydens, and "the curse" was all but forgotten. Will and Azubah's daughters were all married and soon bearing grandchildren regularly. One son, William Henry (known as Henry), was more often than not erratic in nature and was not very dependable. It wasn't long before things started to take a turn for the worse.

The only Hayden eventually left alive was Henry's daughter Armenia. All that was left of her inheritance was an unsavory family reputation and a number of unpaid debts. Due to illness and humiliation, she decided to live out her final days in Waterville, Maine, where she died alone in poverty on February 20, 1927. She was the last of the Hayden family and the final victim of Mercie Dale's curse.

A Canadian family purchased the mansion and land for $25,000. Rumor is that extensive bootlegging now took place within the estate, utilizing a series of underground tunnels previously used for smuggling Chinese laborers. Public dances were held in the old ballroom as the new owners enjoyed their social status. Finally, in 1922, the Canadians sold the property. Over the years, each successive owner found the mansion difficult to maintain in the grand style it was accustomed to. During a period of hard financial times, the estate was sold off piece by piece, barns were burned, the mansion fell into disrepair and the ell (a wing) was engulfed by fire. For many years, the mansion remained abandoned and was open inside and out to anyone passing by.

Stories of ghostly activity and odd lights within the abandoned house were reported by people passing by over the years. Some claim to have heard violin music resonating from the ballroom on a brightly lit, full-moon evening in the summer. An interview with Dwight Dow, a descendant of the family, sets the record straight: "Ghosts? Hell no! Just some drunk passin' by in the middle of the night making up things. They had a ballroom floor, on springs, for dancing, but they weren't no ghosts or none of that. Who's the damn fool that told you that anyway?" Dwight Dow passed away a couple years after the interview, in the late 1970s.

## THE BOORN ULTIMATUM

Jesse Boorn and Stephen Boorn were convicted of murdering a man who was later found alive. The brothers were convicted in 1819, in Manchester, Vermont. The case is the first documented wrongful murder conviction in U.S. history. When Russell Colvin disappeared in 1812, suspicion of foul play fell on his brothers-in-law, Jesse and Stephen Boorn, who never liked Colvin. Seven years later, the uncle of the suspects had a dream in which Colvin appeared to him and said that he had been slain. Colvin did not identify his killers but said that his remains had been buried in a cellar hole on the Boorn farm. The cellar hole was excavated, but no remains were found. Shortly afterward, a dog unearthed some large bones from beneath a nearby stump. Three local physicians examined the bones and declared them human.

Officials took Jesse Boorn into custody. They would have arrested Stephen Boorn as well, but he had moved to New York. While in custody, Jesse's cellmate, forger Silas Merill, told authorities that Jesse confessed. In return for agreeing to testify against Jesse, Merrill was released from jail. Faced with a growing amount of evidence against him, Jesse admitted to the murder but placed principal blame on Stephen, who legally was beyond the reach of the local authorities. A Vermont constable met up with Stephen, and Stephen agreed to return to Vermont with him to clear his name. After his return to Vermont, Stephen confessed as well, claiming to have acted in self-defense.

The local physicians then changed their minds that the found bones were human and declared that they were actually animal remains. Nevertheless, the prosecution pressed ahead with its case, and both of the Boorn brothers were convicted and sentenced to death. The Vermont legislature commuted Jesse's sentence to life in prison but denied relief to Stephen. Shortly before Stephen was to be hanged in 1820, Colvin was found living in New Jersey. On Colvin's return to Vermont, both brothers were released.

## The Town Named After a Cheapskate

Barton, Vermont, is named for Colonel (later General) William Barton, best known for having captured the British commanding general Robert Prescott at Prescott's Rhode Island headquarters in 1777. Prescott's capture lessened the pressure on General George Washington's forces in New Jersey. Barton, Vermont's namesake, later spent fourteen years in jail in Vermont for refusing to pay a public fine, although people who knew him believed he could have easily paid for it.

## Ghosts Still Visit Cahoon Farm

Denise Brown's children swear she didn't tell them about the ghosts before they settled into what, she came to learn, was one of Lyndon's most famous haunted houses. "Maybe that's true," says Brown. "Their father had died, and I was eager to move from Connecticut and didn't feel that a few spirits lingering about should deter us. But in truth, I didn't put much stock into the stories the realtor told me anyway."

The old house had stood empty for several years. The shutters, those that remained, were broken and askew; the shrubs were overgrown, and one door was boarded up against the weather. Dark stains on the ceilings signaled that the roof needed serious repair. The heat and electricity were off, and the air that hung in the dusty rooms was as bitterly cold as that outside.

This is Cahoon Farm, built in 1798. It stayed in the Cahoon-Hoffman family for two centuries. You could say it still is, given its historical importance and occasional nighttime visitors. "Over our five years here, I have come to think that at best we're sharing the property. But I think that's true for anyone who purchases and attempts to preserve a historic home. We become caretakers of the past," says Brown.

We should begin at the beginning, with the story of Daniel Cahoon Sr., who in September 1811 was gored to death while rescuing a child from a bull. Ol' Daniel was laid out in an upstairs bedroom known as the Green Room, and it's his ghost who is said to be heard tromping up the stairs some evenings. And what he's looking for is also the stuff of folklore: a wine cellar supposedly boarded up by his grieving widow, who was convinced it was a potent drink that brought about her husband's demise. People have been searching for that cellar ever since. And so has Daniel, according to legend.

In other stories, overnight visitors have been awakened by ghosts; one supposedly played a bit of tug of war with one guest's blankets, and another held his head in his hands and mourned the drowning of his young son. Clayton Homman, Daniel's descendant who rarely talked about ghosts, is said to have seen one by his bedside—a young woman in old-fashioned dress. Some have heard music playing and glasses tinkling in the parlor that once held the first piano in Lyndon. A young couple dressed for a wedding—the woman in white, the man in a top hat and black jacket—showed up one morning in that upstairs Green Room, which at one time could be expanded into an area fit for ceremonies and balls by lifting up a retractable wall.

"But I have one story to tell. See what you think of this," says Brown. "Shortly after I moved into the house, I decided to have the kitchen countertop replaced. The morning this work was completed, I was standing at the sink, running a dishtowel over the new counter, happy with the job. And I saw a figure float by the kitchen door. She was a bit taller than I, all draped in what seemed to be black lace. And my immediate thought was, "There's the widow of the house checking on the new widow of the house. I stepped into the hallway, but she was gone."

## THE FUR-BEARING TROUT OF LAKE MEMPHREMAGOG

Thinking about going ice fishing in Lake Memphremagog this winter? If so, just maybe you'll catch one of the world-famous fur-bearing trout—trout that are said to grow fur to survive the cold, snowy weather that is so much a part of life in Vermont's Northeast Kingdom (the fur is said to molt off come spring and warmer weather). But don't bet on getting one, because like other creatures said to lurk in the lake that straddles the Vermont/Quebec border, the fur-bearing trout is only a man-made, merry myth passed down through the generations.

How did the myth of the fur-bearing trout arise in the first place? There are several different, yet very similar, stories floating around out there about the origins of this famous species of mythical fish. The following story is the one most often told.

Although Harry Richardson—probably the most prolific photographer to ever live in northern Vermont—gave the trout much-deserved attention, many old-timers in the region point to another long-deceased but lesser-remembered photographer as the mastermind behind the creation of this rare breed of fish. His name was Ralph Sessions, a man who operated a photo studio in Newport, Vermont, a small city located at the

southerly end of Lake Memphremagog. As the story goes, at least the shortened version, Sessions was struck by a humorous idea for a picture while fishing on the international lake: take a perch, wrap it in fur, take a picture of it and make postcards of "the fur-bearing trout."

Some years later, most likely during the 1930s, Sessions sold his studio to Harry Richardson. With Mr. Richardson long departed, it's impossible to know exactly what was in his mind when, seeing Sessions's photos of the fur-bearing trout, he decided to have a taxidermist cover a fish with fur. A picture was taken of Richardson ice fishing on the west side of the lake with Owl's Head looming in the background. Richardson then took that photo, along with the picture of the fur-covered fish (also referred to as a "beaver trout") and produced hundreds, possibly thousands, of postcards. It's almost certainly one of the most recognized postcards in Vermont, if not New England.

No matter how the story behind the fur-bearing trout came to life, the one thing that is certain is that the myth still lives on, and probably will for decades to come.

## RUNAWAY POND

On June 6, 1810, a group of men decided they wanted more water for Aaron Willson's mill in Glover, Vermont. Their plan was to dig a trench at the northern end of Long Pond and allow some of the water to flow south to the Lamoille River. Unfortunately, they weren't aware that the hillside holding back the pond (which was about one hundred feet deep) was composed mostly of quicksand, with a thin layer of "hardpan" that held the water back.

The men proceeded to dig the trench, and the water soon started to sink through the quicksand below. In less than two hours, the pond emptied out completely. It was about noontime that the pond gave way, and the cascade of water made its way toward Lake Memphremagog. By late afternoon, the rush of water had reached Coventry, where it destroyed a bridge at a local farm. No one was injured or killed as one man ran ahead of the flood and was able to warn the mill attendant just in time. The flood was not only water but also trees, branches, dirt and rocks, which gave the man time to get ahead of the entire disaster.

The pathway of the flood for the whole distance from Long Pond to Lake Memphremagog appeared as if swept with a broom of destruction. For many miles, the entire forest was torn up by the roots, and the trees were carried along by the current. At every bend in the stream and on all the land that was not deeply flooded, the trees were left piled up, sometimes to the height of thirty or forty feet. The water in Lake Memphremagog rose about a foot. According to eyewitness Joseph Owen of Barton, the fish in the lake were all swept up the Black River. At Coventry Falls, near to five tons of fish were caught.

## LAKE BOMOSEEN'S GHOSTLY ROWBOAT

The town of West Castleton now sits abandoned, but it was once home to Irish immigrant slate workers who were fond of crossing Lake Bomoseen to visit a tavern on the east shore. One night, three men set out for an eve of carousing. They never returned. The next morning, their boat was found floating empty. Their bodies were never found. Today, lakeside residents claim that sometimes during a full moon, a dark, unoccupied and ghostly rowboat can be seen moving silently across the lake toward the West Castleton bay. No oars disturb the otherwise glassy, still surface.

## DOMESTIC TROUBLES OF THE WORST KIND

As reported in the November 18, 1891 *Rutland Daily Herald*: "Maxim Ramo, who was arrested Monday for assaulting his wife, was tried before Judge Butler yesterday. Ramo told a sorrowful tale of domestic unhappiness and it was evident that he regarded marriage a failure. He said that his wife had tried to shoot him and had also tried to get rid of him by giving him fly powder. He had also done his part towards getting himself out of the way, for he had tried to hang himself but the rope broke. Mrs. Ramo then told her story and it was supported by several witnesses. The Judge fined Ramo $13.51 and gave him some good advice." Whether he followed that advice or not is unknown.

## ON THE TURNING AWAY

At the Austine School for the Deaf, security guards report that they have heard their names called when there was absolutely no one else around. Other staff members have been beckoned to the same spot, all on different occasions. Other reports include a variety of strange noises. Occasionally, "something" will pass by, momentarily visible just out of the corner of your eye. Lights turn on by themselves. A sense that you are being followed is not uncommon. When you turn around, nothing is there. Eerie shadows or apparitions sometimes become visible on the screens of televisions that are turned off. Fortunately, no malevolent activity has ever been reported. Perhaps the ghostly residents are simply curious or concerned about the everyday activities at the school.

## THE "BENNINGTON TRIANGLE"

The term "Bennington Triangle" was coined by Vermont author Joseph A. Citro during a public radio broadcast in 1992 to denote an area of southwestern Vermont within which a number of persons went missing between 1920 and 1950.

Bennington is located in southern Vermont and is the third largest town in the state. Primarily known for the Battle of Bennington, the region is rich in historical events dating back to the 1700s. Bennington is fertile ground for ghostly events, folklore and supernatural occurrences. The region is often referred to as the "Bennington Triangle" due to the many odd, unexplained happenings within its surroundings, buildings and nearby mountains. American Indians considered Glastenbury Mountain "cursed" and used it strictly for burying their dead. Locals believed the American Indians and avoided it for that reason, and for tales of hairy "wild men" and other strange beasts in the woods. They believed the land to be cursed because all four winds met in that spot. There is also mention in American Indian folklore of an enchanted stone, which is said to swallow anything that steps on it.

Over the years, there have been between thirty and forty unexplained disappearances on the mountain. It is known for certain that at least five persons from this area went missing, some of them on Glastenbury Mountain itself, between 1945 and 1950. These include seventy-four-year-old Middie Rivers, sixty-eight-year-old James Tedford, eight-year-old Paul Jepson, eighteen-year-old Paula Welden and fifty-three-year-old Frieda Langer. Of these, the remains of only one were found, those of Frieda Langer.

Most reports on the subject view the circumstances as mysterious, as her body turned up in some tall grasses in an area that had been searched extensively a number of times in the seven months between her disappearance and the discovery of the corpse, making it unlikely that the search teams had simply missed her. There were several strange circumstances surrounding these disappearances.

In 1892, a millworker named Henry MacDowell killed his co-worker, Jim Crowley, in a drunken fight. He was sentenced to life in an asylum but escaped, never to be seen again.

Seventy-five-year-old Middie Rivers lived in the region all his life and was with a group of four hunters. When the group was returning to camp, near Long Trail Road and Route 9, he got slightly ahead of them, and no one ever saw him again. Volunteers searched the area for the experienced woodsman, but he was never found. The only remaining clue was a single bullet that his friends speculated might have fallen out of his belt when Rivers took a drink of water.

On December 1, 1946, Paula Welden, an eighteen-year-old sophomore at Bennington College, went on what was supposed to be a short hike on the Long Trail but vanished without a trace. She hitched a ride to the Long Trail, and several witnesses confirmed seeing her on the trail, but after not returning to school, a search was conducted. Despite a $5,000 reward, Paula Welden was never seen again.

Jim Tedford was on a bus that he had boarded in St. Albans with other people. No one saw him get off at the Bennington Soldiers Home where he lived. He was simply gone. His presence on the bus was confirmed at the stop before Bennington, but he was not on the bus when it reached Bennington. None of the passengers, including the driver, had any idea what happened to him. Jim's disappearance was also on the third anniversary of Paula Welden's disappearance.

On October 12, 1950, eight-year-old Paul Jepson became another probable victim of the Bennington Triangle. His mother was tending to some pigs, leaving Paul unattended for no more than an hour, only to later find him gone without a trace. According to the boy's father, Paul had a strange compulsion to go into the mountains on occasion. Paul was wearing a red jacket, which would have made him more visible, but thorough search parties found nothing. Bloodhounds traced his scent to a highway and suddenly lost it, suggesting that Paul was picked up or simply vanished, never to be found.

Two weeks after Paul disappeared, on October 28, Frieda Langer disappeared. She was hiking with her cousin and simply walked just out of sight to change her clothes after falling into a stream. When she didn't return, her cousin went back to camp only to discover that she had never arrived, and nobody saw her leave the woods. Frieda Langer was an experienced woodsman and gun handler. She knew the area well and was unlikely to get lost, especially since it was still broad daylight. Search teams scoured the area on foot, by plane and by helicopter but found nothing. Another search on November 5 and 7 turned up nothing at all. And on November 11 and 12, three hundred military, police, firemen, sportsmen and volunteers also came up empty-handed. On May 12, 1951, Langer's body did turn up, in an open area where she would not have been missed during the search. The cause of death was unknown.

Frances Christman vanished on a half-mile hike to a friend's house. Because of the wide range of ages and genders of the missing persons, it is thought that their being victims of a serial killer is unlikely. This, combined with a lack of any evidence to offer support for any more prosaic explanation, has led many to speculate on possible paranormal causes, including abduction by UFO occupants, "cross dimensional wormholes" or attack by the "Bennington Monster."

The trails stop partially up the mountain, suggesting that no one goes up there. When you walk into the woodlands of Glastenbury Mountain, you don't hear anything living; it's as though even the animals don't dare to venture there.

## SLIPPERYSKIN—BEAR, BIGFOOT OR INDIAN?

In the 1700s, the Northeast Kingdom of Vermont was (and still is to a certain degree) frontier country. It was inhabited by woodsmen, hunters, trappers, fishermen, extended families and Wabanaki (mostly) but also a few sturdy others. It is told that it was also the haunt of "Slipperyskin," a bear that is supposed to have caused a general misery among the settlers. He was named Slipperyskin because he managed to elude every trap that was ever set for him. The American Indians knew him and called him "Wejuk" or "Wet Skin."

The story is told that an old bear once terrorized Lemington, Vermont, for many years and committed wholesale destruction. He was a mean animal and evidently had a grudge against humans. He destroyed their fences, ripped up their gardens, frightened their cows and sheep, tromped through the cornfields and caused no end of mayhem.

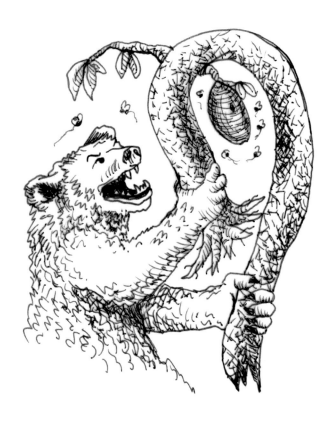

He was a huge bear, the stories relate, and he always ran on his hind legs and never on all fours. Before a hunter could lay his gun sights on him, the old bear would vanish into the woods as silently and swiftly as a drift of smoke. He is said to have left tracks as big as wagon wheels, and for what it is worth, it is told he squeezed the sap out of maple trees when he felt so inclined. For maliciousness and cunning, it was claimed he could never be compared, except to humans. He seemed to enjoy himself immensely, frightening people and livestock, kicking over manure piles and throwing stones into machinery left in fields. Where the old bear came from, and why he eventually disappeared entirely, is a mystery.

## GHOSTS OF UVM

Burlington is Vermont's largest city, and the University of Vermont is the state's largest university. Perhaps that helps to explain why it is also one of the most active hotspots of supernatural activity. It seems that the number of ghosts within the halls of UVM may sometimes rival the head count of the living student body, easily earning it the title of "Most Haunted College in Vermont."

The following are a sample of some of the spine-tingling events that have taken place within the walls of the university.

The agriculture department (Bittersweet House) has a female ghost in period dress, circa late nineteenth century, who unexpectedly makes her appearance known. The Center for Cultural Pluralism (Allen House) reportedly has a ghost taking up residence on the top floor. Although he (or she) hasn't been seen visually, a cold presence can be felt in the vicinity.

The Center for Counseling and Testing is rumored to be haunted. The former director encountered the ghost of Captain Jacobs, a retired seaman who died there in the early part of the twentieth century. Poltergeist activity, which is often described as "noisy ghost" activity, has been reported there as recently as 1992. It would seem that Captain Jacobs is a restless spirit indeed!

The Grasse Mount House comes with a vibrant though eerie history of ghostly voices and doors that slam and lock themselves without human effort. Converse Hall is reportedly haunted by a former student who committed suicide there. Though never seen, the student remains as active in death as he may have been while he was one of the living. He turns radios on and off and interacts with electrical equipment. The student electrocuted himself in 1998.

## THE TRAGIC STORY OF ELI CORTI

According to the *Barre Daily Times* of October 5, 1903, "Eli Corti was shot in the stomach and mortally wounded at a meeting in the Socialist building on Granite Street. Corti died at midnight last night at Heaton Hospital in Montpelier having lived about thirty hours after he received the bullet. The shooting occurred at 7:15 PM on Saturday evening and was the outcome of a general discussion between the socialists and anarchists present. Andrew Garetto was arrested and charged with the shooting. Garetto was sentenced to serve not less than ten nor more than twelve years in state prison."

On his release, Garetto returned to Barre but left shortly after, and it is believed that he went back to Italy. Eli Corti and his monument are very much a part of the story of memorial art at Hope Cemetery in Barre, Vermont. Cut from a single piece of granite by the brother of the deceased, the outstanding, hand-carved, life-sized figure sits quietly contemplative. The detail of the clothing and the tools of the granite trade almost bring this figure to life.

## A Name Unique Throughout the World

St. Johnsbury, Vermont, was named for Michel Guillaume Jean de Crèvecoeur, also known as J. Hector St. John, author of *Letters from an American Farmer*. St. John was a friend to Washington and Franklin, as well as a correspondent of Ethan Allen, and had an enthusiasm both for the Republic of Vermont and for place names. He suggested the names Vergennes, Danville and St. Johnsbury. Realizing that several places already bore the name of St. John, J. Hector suggested the longer name, St. Johnsbury, which remains the only place with that name in the world. St. John became a naturalized citizen of the new country, and in 1793, he was appointed to the post of French consul in New York City.

## Elementary School Apparitions

Sightings of ghostly figures have been witnessed in the Johnson Elementary School. Some have reported that apparitions can be seen peering through the windows of the 1895 historic schoolhouse, which was renovated in 1997. The old tower is said to be the most haunted area of the building. A ringing bell in the tower has been heard by many people. Janitors have heard footsteps traveling through the halls, faint laughs of children and doors shutting and have felt the temperature dropping rapidly.

## RESTAURANT GHOST

The story goes that a man who once worked at the former Carburs Restaurant building (now known as American Flatbread) killed himself in the basement. The bullet went through his head and into a nearby wall. Supposedly, you can still see the bullet hole in the basement. Most ghostly encounters happen in the basement, which houses the kitchen and tapped kegs under the bar. Waitresses reported their skirts being lifted up from a cold wind. Doors have slammed closed, trapping employees in the basement's walk-in freezer. Waitresses were told not to go down to the basement. The basement is also connected to other old buildings in downtown Burlington by various tunnels from the Prohibition era. There are a lot of reports of phantom voices heard throughout the restaurant when no one is there. The ghost seems to specifically taunt women. Reports of breaking glasses, plates flying off counters and suddenly increased oven temperatures were not uncommon. A female bartender reported a pyramid of water glasses appearing on the bar, right after she had put the glasses away and turned her back for a second.

## A BLOODY RELIC

On December 26, 1861, the *Vermont Phoenix* reported the following during times of the Civil War: "Private John Wheeler of Company F, 4th Vermont Volunteers, has sent to one of his friends in this village a piece of a newspaper stained with the heart's blood of the first deserter and traitor shot by order of our military officers." This "memorial" was posted in Lilley's saloon in Brattleboro, Vermont.

## VAMPIRES IN VERMONT?

A vampire's heart burned on the village green in Woodstock, Vermont? Maybe. There is a well-known legend that suggests that, in 1834, the eldest son of the Corwin family of Woodstock, Vermont, died from a mysterious wasting disease. When another son became ill, townspeople of Woodstock advised the Corwins to take precautions against a vampire. According to legend, the eldest brother was disinterred from the Cushing Cemetery and burned. His ashes were buried in an iron container beneath the Woodstock village green. Supposedly, a few local boys decided to get together late one night and dig up the burned ashes. They quickly abandoned their grisly task when they heard unearthly screams and voices all around them. This all may be typical New England folklore, as the town register does not contain any records about a Corwin family who were born, died or held land plots in the Woodstock community.

## THE OLD STONE HOUSE

According to lore, when the Reverend Alexander Lucius Twilight—the first black college graduate in the United States—asked the board of trustees to build a dorm for the students of the Brownington Academy, it refused. So, he built one himself using extraordinary methods, including a staging platform that rose as an ox turned a treadmill. As the building rose, so did the ox and the treadmill. And, since there was no way to get the ox back down when the building was completed, it was slaughtered for a great feast of celebration.

## Spirits Roam the Halls at St. Michael's College

There are a couple of places on campus that seem to have ghostly visitors. Herrouet Theater, now a run-down building used for storage, is supposedly haunted by a nun who died in the 1950s. Her spirit, some say, has never left the building.

The men's first-year dormitory is said to contain an evil presence. In the sixties or seventies, young men were rumored to be holding some sort of occult meetings. One of the men insisted that he needed to close the "portal" before they left, but security arrived and tossed them off campus before they could complete the ritual. The door to the attic is padlocked shut. However, lights go on in the attic, and footsteps are heard in the middle of the night by the residents on the top floor. The image of the pentagram still exists on the floor despite attempts to replace the wood.

## Hole in the Head

Phineas Gage began the day of September 13, 1848, as a man remarkable only to those who knew him personally. He worked as the foreman of a railway construction gang in Vermont, where his group was preparing the bed for the Rutland and Burlington Railroad. Gage's job was to remove large sections of rock by shattering it from the inside out.

Gage had drilled a hole into a rock and filled it with powder, indicating to the man helping him that it was time to fill in the sand. At that point, someone called to Gage, and he must have become distracted. He failed to notice that his colleague had not yet added the sand to the hole and began tamping directly onto the explosive powder. Almost immediately the sparks struck fire in the hole, and the charge blew up in Gage's face. The force of the explosion drove his three-foot-long iron rod at high speed into Gage's left cheekbone, through his skull and out the top of his head. It landed nearly three hundred feet away.

Amazingly, Gage survived the terrible blow. Witnesses reported that while he was thrown to the ground and exhibited a few convulsions, he was alert and rational within a few minutes after the accident. Miraculously, Gage suffered no motor or speech impairments as a result of his accident. His memory was intact, and he gradually regained his physical strength. His personality underwent a dramatic shift, changing his disposition to such a degree that his friends barely recognized him. "Gage," they said, "was no longer Gage."

When Gage died in 1861, there was no autopsy performed, so no one was able to verify the exact brain regions damaged in his accident. Fortunately, for later researchers, a Dr. Harlow had Gage's body exhumed in 1866, at which point the skull and the tamping iron he was buried with went to the Warren Medical Museum of Harvard Medical School, where they have remained ever since.

## RESIDENT GHOSTS OF THE BACK INN TIME

Friendly resident ghosts are said to make the Back Inn Time (a local inn in St. Albans, Vermont) their home. There is Lora, the wife of Sidney Weaver, a past owner of the home. Lora died at the young age of thirty; however, her spirit lives on at Back Inn Time. Another ghost spotted is that of a man. He has been seen in the downstairs parlor.

Many guests claimed to have heard voices, noises or even seen apparitions while staying at the inn. Built in 1858 by Victor Attwood, the building has seen some rich history. Despite only one man being documented as dying in the building, patrons claim to see an older woman. The man who passed away was a descendant of Victor Attwood and was the last owner in the family until it was purchased by the current owners. Besides that, it has been claimed by psychics that the land was once used as a site for child slavery. There is also mention of a mentally challenged person being locked in a windowless room within the inn.

## Lake Memphremagog Monster

The first nonfictional document describing the sightings of a creature in Lake Memphremagog dates back to 1816 and is signed by Ralph Merry IV. He describes four experiences as related by the citizens of Georgeville, Quebec, which he found to be totally credible. He, however, was not a witness to any of these phenomena but only reported the facts as he knew them. The descriptions usually coincide as to the length and appearance of the serpent-like creature.

To date, more than 215 sightings have been reported and documented with great care. Each account is signed and recorded. Hearsay accounts are simply refused. There have been, on average, 8 sightings annually, which have been confirmed by about twenty witnesses. In 1961, two fishermen heading for Newport, Vermont, observed for about forty seconds a black creature, about twenty feet long, swimming partially submerged. According to these men, the creature that was about two hundred feet from their boat had a round back and an indescribable head. This scene was accompanied by a strange sound. Additional sightings have been reported up until 1996. Many locals who have lived in the area all of their lives discount the stories as myth and nonsense.

From surveying recorded accounts, speaking with local people and viewing video of the alleged monster, it is only possible to conclude that the idea of such a lake monster is a social construct, born of native mythology and tradition and kept alive by local people for fun and tourism potential. The mythological creature is not universally recognized as being "real" to the people who live around the lake. It has the air of a favorite mascot.

The general view is that if there is anything biological in the lake at all, it is a giant eel or sturgeon. Most of the sightings are of boat wakes that do strange things on their own, without any input from the "Memphremagog Monster."

## CATHOUSE FOLLIES

Colonel Thomas had some very spirited new recruits to contend with during the Civil War. Perhaps he didn't realize the difficult task of converting Vermont farmers' sons into soldiers. From the *Vermont Phoenix*, February 27, 1862: "Late on Saturday evening the police of this village were called upon to suppress a disturbance at a house of ill-repute on Flat-street [in Brattleboro, Vermont], occasioned by some of the soldiers of the 8th Regiment. The police declined to interfere unless accompanied by some of the proper military authorities. Accordingly the information was laid before Col. Thomas who, with suitable guard, proceeded to the aforesaid establishment and there captured a happy Lieutenant and sundry privates. The captive officer was ordered to report himself under arrest and the privates were sent to the guard house. Two of the privates escaped with one of the women by secreting themselves in the cellar. It is currently reported that these arrests were made upon information given by certain civilians, who had been temporarily supplanted in the affections of the inmates of this house by the aforementioned soldiers."

## The Wicked Witch of the North

In 1879, Hetty Green was a mean-spirited, tightfisted and shrewd woman who lived in Bellows Falls. In New York City, she was known as the "Witch of Wall Street" and the world's richest woman, even though she decided to stay in cheap boardinghouses. Her simple Quaker dress, frugal lifestyle and great wealth inevitably made her a unique and conspicuous person wherever she lived.

Hetty always lived as she wanted: frugally and independently. She would walk to the grocery store at the south end of Atkinson Street, where she bought broken cookies in bulk, considerably less expensive. She returned her berry boxes for a nickel. She carried a small milk can to get the best price on milk for her cat. She would get a free bone for her dog with her purchases. She is said to have once spent hours searching for a two-cent stamp she had lost.

Even Hetty's son, Ned, was the recipient of her mean-spirited cheapness. When he injured his knee, Hetty refused to pay for a doctor and treated the injury herself. Two years later, when her son's knee still hadn't healed, Hetty dressed him in rags and pretended to be a charity case. When the doctor learned who she was and demanded payment, Hetty left his office in a rage. Several years later, the boy's leg had to be amputated.

Children ran when she walked down the street because they had seen long black skirts such as she always wore only in pictures of witches. When the bottom of the skirt needed to be washed from all the dust and dirt it swept through, she went to Wheeler's Laundry in the square, where she instructed them to "wash only the bottom." She waited in her ample petticoats until her skirt was ready for her.

On her seventy-eighth birthday, she said her good health and long life were possible because of her habit of chewing baked onions. Hetty herself lived off cold oatmeal because she was too stingy to heat it, and she died of apoplexy in an argument over the virtues of skimmed milk. Hetty's last years were spent in New York. She had had several strokes and was confined to a wheelchair. She died at Ned's unpretentious house on West Ninetieth Street. The year was 1916, and she left behind every penny of some $100 million (equal to about $1.5 billion today). Friendless and pathetic, Hetty Green was reputedly the wealthiest woman in the United States at that time.

## SUPERNATURAL SOUTHERN VERMONT

Southern Vermont College is located on Mount Anthony, also in Bennington, Vermont. There you will find amazing photos of supernatural images and statues. The college was a former seminary that was closed and turned into a coed campus. Reports from students and night security officers include a number of eerie events that defy a rational explanation. For example, apparitions have been seen in the house. These include Everett (the original owner of the house), his wife and a person in a black-hooded robe. Odd occurrences are almost the norm, such as smoke-filled hallways, lights turning on in rooms that are locked, doors and windows unlocked after being locked during a previous security round and footsteps all around the college when no one else is in the building.

There is also a ghostly history behind one of the computer labs that used to be the old carriage house.

The doors of the building sometimes lock by themselves, and computers have been known to act oddly, sometimes shutting off on their own. Wandering about the main building, witnesses have claimed, is the ghost of a man who is dressed in period attire. The two most active haunting spots in this mansion are on the third floor, where the Abbey Room is burning with energy. Now a classroom, it was the sleeping quarters for the house staff, where a maid allegedly hanged herself.

## WHERE CAN YOU VISIT A BORED ANGEL?

Carver Louis Brusa created an angel headstone—which rests between columns with her legs crossed and her head balanced on her chin—at the Hope Cemetery in Barre. Brusa's own grave features a strange sculpture of *The Dying Man*, slipping away, held by his wife. Brusa succumbed in 1937 to a common stone carver's ailment, silicosis, from a lifetime of sucking in airborne stone particles.

## FLIGHTS OF FANCY

From *Aurora of the Valley* (a newspaper in Windsor, Vermont) on December 21, 1872: "The story goes that a boy way back in 1811 made a kite and attached a paper lantern to it, in which he put a candle, and arranged it so that when the candle had burned out it would explode some powder which was in the bottom of the lantern. He kept the secret to himself, and waited for a suitable night in which to raise his kite. The boy got his kite into the air without being discovered, for it was so dark that nothing but the colored lantern was visible. It went dancing about in the air wildly, attracting much notice, and was looked upon by ignorant people as some supernatural omen. The evil spirit, as many supposed it, went bobbling around for about twenty minutes and then exploded, blowing the lantern to pieces. Next morning all was wonder and excitement, and this lad, who had taken his kite and hidden it after the explosion without being found out, had his own fun out of the matter. The people of Brattleboro never had any explanation of the mystery until nearly sixty years afterward, when the boy who had become quite an old gentleman, published the story in a Brattleboro newspaper."

## GHOSTLY HAPPENINGS

In the 1960s, five Winooski High School students were killed in a crash coming back from Canada after a suspected night of drinking. The local funeral home didn't have enough room in its parlors to hold all five bodies, so the others were laid out in the school gym. A mass wake was later held there. Janitors have reported strange sightings since then up to the present day when cleaning late at night, especially after sporting events. Ghostly happenings include lights flicking on and off, lockers mysteriously opening and slamming shut all down the hall, echoing voices in the gym and so forth. But perhaps most frightening is the sound of wheels rolling along the gym floor, echoing the coffins being rolled into the gym for the wake.

## SNOWFLAKE BENTLEY

Do you remember hearing the phrase "no two snowflakes are alike"? This is a true fact and not just a saying. The discovery was actually made in the small rural town of Jericho, Vermont, by Wilson A. Bentley. Bentley was always fascinated with snowflakes and was stunned by their beauty when, at age fifteen, he was given a microscope by his mother.

Bentley, a farmer who was educated at home, attracted worldwide attention with his pioneering work in the area of photomicrography, most notably his extensive work with snow crystals, commonly known as snowflakes. By adapting a microscope to a bellows camera, and after years of trial and error, he became the first to photograph a single snow crystal in 1885.

Bentley would go on to capture thousands of snowflakes during his lifetime, not finding any two alike. His snow crystal photomicrographs were acquired by colleges and universities throughout the world. He published numerous articles for magazines and journals, including *Scientific American* and *National Geographic*. At the age of sixty-six, a book of his work was published, which brought the beauty of snow to people throughout the world.

On December 23, 1931, Bentley died at the family farmhouse in Jericho. Because of his wonderful work with snow crystals, he became affectionately known as "Snowflake" Bentley and was known as the world's expert on snowflakes.

## Brass Lantern Inn's Ghostly Guests

Word has it that one of this inn's rooms is occupied, even when no living guest is spending the night there. A number of visitors, as well as the inn's staff, have heard the voices of enthused spirits talking about a dance they attended. Of course, when the room is checked for interlopers, no one is there.

An innkeeper gave an example of a guest who asked about the "people who came in late last night talking loud enough so I could hear their words? And where did they go to a party?" And another guest mentioned that he "heard the people across the hall from me last night talking and laughing and speaking about how happy they were." In each of these instances, it's in reference to the same room, always late at night and with similar descriptions as to what they heard the other guests saying. Oddly enough, there were no guests across the hall.

## Swimming Hole of Death

Thousands of people head to the Huntington River Gorge every summer. But many lives have been lost in one popular spot, and its frightening death toll has continued to climb over the last half century. A sign at the falls indicates the tragic fates of twenty-two visitors since 1950. With some common sense and some careful scouting, visitors can bypass the obvious dangers at the gorge, enjoy the popular swimming holes and marvel at the gorge and falls. Huntington Gorge has developed a reputation as a killer. It is estimated that over forty people have drowned in the gorge. Deadly as it may be, it is a beautiful place and just requires a bit of caution and common sense.

## GRAVE ROBBING YOUR WAY TO SUCCESS

John Pearl Gifford was, to all appearances, an esteemed young man. He was an 1894 Phi Beta Kappa graduate of Dartmouth College and the valedictorian of the Dartmouth Medical School class of 1897. In 1903, he founded a hospital in Randolph, Vermont. So what are latter-day observers to make of the fact that he was also a convicted grave robber?

John Gifford grew up on a farm in Randolph, Vermont, and achieved academic glory at nearby Dartmouth before returning to practice medicine in his hometown. However, shortly before collecting his MD, he was charged (along with a fellow student) of grave robbing. According to the *Granite State Free Press*, the body of one Joseph Murdock was discovered to be missing from his grave when members of his family noticed footprints in the snow—tracks leading across the cemetery straight for a road. Despicable though the idea of stealing the bodies of the poor and disenfranchised may seem (the rich were not at risk of "body snatching," for they could afford to purchase secure burial vaults or to post guards at a grave site until a disinterment would not yield a body of any use to a medical school), the practice was considered by medical educators to be quite justifiable.

Ultimately, Gifford and his accomplice were convicted and fined for the crime, which was paid for on their behalf by the faculty of the medical school. Gifford went on to greater success and founded a hospital, the Gifford Medical Center, in Randolph, Vermont.

## VERMONT-STYLE "POP-SICLES"

Vermonters are a frugal bunch and have been for many generations. In order to save energy during a long, cold Vermont winter, the truly ingenious old-time Vermont natives would find a way to conserve food and heat by

freezing their old folks for the duration of winter and thawing them out in the springtime!

"A Strange Tale," describing this unbelievable ritual, was published on the front page of the *Montpelier Argus and Patriot* on December 21, 1887. The story, reported to be true, tells of a poor, northern Vermont family who had established the idea of putting their elderly and weakest family members into cold storage until they could be thawed out just in time for spring planting.

Times change, and the old traditions have a way of fading out. These days, we Vermonters just buy an extra pair of woolen socks and throw an extra blanket or two on top of grandpa.

## THE EQUINOX GHOST STORY

Mary Todd Lincoln and her children from Washington, D.C., spent two summers at the Equinox Resort, built in 1769, in Manchester Village, Vermont. The family planned to return in the summer of 1865, but plans changed after the assassination of Abraham Lincoln. The family's ties to the area continued and strengthened with son Robert Todd Lincoln's purchase of neighboring estate Hildene. Employees at the hotel report seeing images on the third floor of a woman and a child that are consistent with descriptions of Mary Todd Lincoln and one of her sons. Perhaps through their visits they are trying to recapture the carefree days of those summers.

Two housekeepers encountered a spirit while they were cleaning the two-story-high Green Mountain Suite. The housekeepers made the beds on the first floor and then split up to make the upstairs beds. When the housekeepers returned downstairs, they found that the blankets and pillows had been ripped off the beds they had just made, and blankets had been thrown around the room. The identity of this ghost is a mystery.

## VERMONT POLICE ACADEMY'S GHOSTLY NURSE

In 1907, the Vermont Police Academy was a state hospital for tuberculosis patients called the Vermont Sanatorium. It became the Vermont Police Academy in 1971. To this day, the building is haunted by a nurse who worked at the hospital. While there, she reportedly contracted the disease herself. All of the old call buttons are still in the recruits' rooms. It is said that, if pushed, the friendly ghost of the nurse, Mary, will pay a visit during the night.

## HIGH SPIRITS AT THE INN

The Highgate Manor was built in 1818, by Captain Steve Keyes, along with the Manor Mayfair, which was located directly across the green from the Highgate Manor. During the Civil War, the manor was used as a stop on the underground railroad, with tunnels running from under the house to the river. These tunnels are still in existence today under the manor.

The Keyes family owned the manor until the year 1870, when the home was sold to Dr. Henry Baxter. As was the custom of the day, Dr. Baxter opened his practice in his home, the Highgate Manor. Bloodstains from his operating table are still visible on the wood floor in what is now the library. It was during this time that the legend of the Highgate Manor started to grow. Many of Dr. Baxter's children did not live past the age of ten and died of strange illnesses. The townspeople believed that the good doctor was using his children for experiments and that after their death they have since remained in the house to this day.

After the death of Dr. Baxter in 1898, the manor was taken over by Philip Schmitt; in 1917, the manor was turned into an exclusive vacation resort. With business becoming an incredible success, Manor Mayfair was again added as part of the Highgate Manor estate, along with the Manor Annex and a brand-new dance hall. This hall was billed as the largest and best dance hall in the North. Due to the exclusivity of the manor, Al Capone, as well as many other high-profile dignitaries, frequented the manor estate and its speakeasy hidden in a cave beneath the grounds.

The manor continued as a vacation destination during the 1940s. During this time, Benny Goodman and other stars of the big-band era regularly performed in the manor's ballroom specifically added for this purpose. Unfortunately, on May 22, 1950, part of the Highgate Manor's estate, the Manor Mayfair, was destroyed by a fire set when a worker started burning leaves too close to Mayfair.

Guests often report a strange presence in the basement bar (named after past visitor Al Capone). Ghostly voices have been heard, and some believe that the ghosts of Dr. Baxter's children still haunt the inn.

## CROSSES BURNED IN VERMONT

Although many refuse to discuss it, or even acknowledge the fact, it is true that Vermont history includes a period of involvement with the Ku Klux Klan. At the time, in the 1920s, some of Vermont's leading citizens were certainly included among its numbers. In St. Johnsbury, the minister of the Congregational church delivered a sermon on "The Psychology of the Ku Klux Klan," in which he reasoned that the cross burnings and bonfire rallies must have some justification or else they would not have caught on so rapidly. Soon, there were enough members there to get a legal charter and stage a public meeting in a field outside of town where over two thousand Klansmen gathered, most in full regalia, many with faces covered. Similar gatherings took place in Windsor, Springfield and elsewhere. By the mid-twenties, more than fourteen thousand Vermonters in Chittenden, Washington, Orange and Caledonia Counties had paid the ten-dollar initiation fee, making the Klan a force to be reckoned with politically. Calvin Coolidge, running for president, stated that he was not a member of the KKK, but "Silent Cal" was true to form in refusing to condemn the Klan by name. And while several towns, including Burlington, passed local ordinances that forbade wearing masks in public, for the purpose of reining in the Klan's activities, a similar statewide statute was killed in the senate in Montpelier.

## THE DOG-LOVING GHOST OF ST. JOHNSBURY ACADEMY

Brantview House, which was once a private residence, is reputedly haunted by a dog-loving ghost. One evening, the house mother was reading in the parlor when her beloved Afghan, resting at her feet, suddenly began snarling. She noticed the dog's fur was gently ruffled by an unseen, ghostly hand. The animal immediately relaxed and watched as the spectral visitor politely left the room.

## ONE-DOLLAR REWARD

An ad in a newspaper in Brattleboro, Vermont, on September 21, 1798, read: "Ran away from the subscriber, on the 19th instant, in indented boy, named SAMUEL BRIGGS, about 17 years of age, has light blue eyes, a large mouth, throws back his head and shows his teeth when he laughs; had on when he went away, a checked woollen shirt, brown tow cloth trowsers, and a striped bottle green waistcoat. Whosoever will take up said runaway, and return him to the subscriber, will be entitled to the above reward, but no charges. All persons are forbid harbouring or trusting said boy—thus they will avoid the penalty of the law."

## BURLINGTON CITY HAUNTS

The Firehouse Gallery next to city hall is rumored to be haunted by a firefighter who died on the job in 1877.

Workers at the nearby Flynn Theater have reported seeing the ghost of a long-deceased employee floating through the air. And then there's the bone-chilling story surrounding the majestic Pomerleau building overlooking Burlington's waterfront, which is supposedly haunted by a previous owner who lost his mind.

## THE PIGMAN

In 1971, a farmer in Northfield, Vermont, went to investigate some strange noises coming from his backyard one night. He turned on his outside light and peered out the kitchen window, expecting to see a raccoon or plump squirrel sifting through his garbage. Instead, he met the gaze of a man-sized figure lurking along the edges of the yellow light. His body was covered in white hair, and he had the facial features of a pig. A few seconds later, the figure darted back into the shadows. A few days passed before the "Pigman" was spotted again, this time by a group of students outside the high school during a dance. Reports are vague as to who ran away faster—the students or the creature—but both quickly left the scene. Since these initial sightings, the Pigman has become a sort of rural legend in Northfield, and more than one

nighttime traveler has claimed he encountered the Pigman while driving his car along a deserted country road, the hairy white beast narrowly missing the front end of the vehicle.

## LEGEND OF "JOHNNY SEESAW"

Johnny Seesaw's was built in 1920 by Russian logger Ivan Sesow. Sesow called his enterprise "The Wonderview Log

Pavilion" and began the legend with his wild Saturday night dances, homemade moonshine and rumored sin cabins out back. Throughout the Roaring Twenties, thanks to Prohibition, a few lawmen and many loggers, "the Legend of Johnny Seesaw's" continued to grow. About 1930, Sesow apparently bet the dance hall in one of his famous poker games, and lost. The buildings were sold and remained unused for some eight years.

In 1938, Bill and Mary Parrish bought the run-down property; constructed bunkrooms; installed plumbing, electricity, a kitchen and a central furnace; and renamed one of the first ski lodges in the United States "Johnny Seesaw's." For the next four decades, Johnny Seesaw's catered to thousands of skiers, including a president of the United States, Charles Lindbergh (the first aviator to cross the Atlantic) and a bevy of famous and infamous personalities. At the beginning of World War II, the concept of army ski troops originated at Johnny Seesaw's and eventually became the Tenth Mountain Division. For forty years, Seesaw's, a renowned Ivy League hangout, offered lodging by referral only. If you didn't know someone who had stayed there, you didn't stay there.

## FRIENDLY GHOSTS

Travelers on the Old Silo Road in East Barnet will find signs leading to Inwood Manor, a former stagecoach stop, croquet factory, dorm and bed-and-breakfast inn. Although the building has been closed for many years, certain "guests" apparently still check in. While a bed-and-breakfast, guests told the owner of seeing disembodied hands and hearing music coming from a grand piano that was locked in a private room. Some believe that several owners were monks.

A woman and her small child drowned in the Connecticut River, near the inn. The process of renovating any building often stirs up ghosts living there. After the owners started renovating this thirty-two-room inn, a friendly, smiling female apparition, dressed in a candy-striped dress, appeared to them to offer a gracious welcome and to encourage their efforts. She was obviously pleased that they were repairing and renovating her inn, the place where she sought refuge after her unfortunate accident. After she appeared at the foot of the stairs before them, she turned around, floated up the stairs and then melted into thin air. They knew then that they had their first customer/resident, even if she was a ghost. This friendly, benign female apparition turned out not to be alone. The apparition of her little child, who drowned with her, appeared before the owners soon afterward.

## GHOSTS APLENTY

The Norwich Inn, with connecting microbrewery, was built over two hundred years ago. It also appears to be the home of a substantial number of ghosts. One of the ghosts, a woman wearing a long black skirt, is said to have been seen gliding through the building's parlor and on into the adjoining library. Other phenomena include toilets flushing by themselves, water faucets turning off and on and chairs rocking eerily by themselves with no one sitting in them.

## WATERBURY'S OLD STAGECOACH INN

Room 2 is said to be haunted by Margaret Spencer, who died there. Built in 1826 by a wealthy millionaire, it has served as a tavern, a stagecoach stop and a private residence and is now one of Waterbury's most well-known historic inns.

During the period between the 1920s and the 1940s, the Old Stagecoach Inn was the private residence of a wealthy socialite, Margaret Spencer. In 1947, Margaret died at the age of ninety-eight, in her own bedroom, which is now room 2. Margaret Spencer loved her home so much that she didn't pass over to the other side. Instead, she decided to hang around her old bedroom, appearing to startled guests and wearing a white shawl. Margaret has no plans to leave, and the current owners have made no effort to make her do so. She seems to be willing to share her room with the living, though the living may be a little unsure about sharing a room with a ghostly presence.

Ghostly incidents are mostly minor (similar to practical jokes), as though someone or something was having fun with a bewildered housekeeper or guest. Such events would often occur in broad daylight with people present and at other times in the dead of night. But never is there anything sinister or malicious involved. For example, a rocking chair will suddenly begin to rock in an agitated manner and will continue for several minutes with no one near it; furniture items are moved, beds have their linens stripped and neatly folded while the housekeeper is working nearby and other similar incidents occur that are too numerous to mention. There has been a reluctance of cleaning staff to work alone upstairs, even though they're probably not alone. Margaret Spencer is almost certain to be keeping them company.

## NORWICH UNIVERSITY'S GHOSTLY CADETS

At Alumni Hall, one of the dorms, a cadet hanged himself a few years back. A couple years later, his brother attended Norwich, lived in the same room and hanged himself, too. Now the room is boarded off. Chaplin Hall is haunted by an unknown spirit visible at night by the front door. When the building was used as a library, books regularly floated off shelves, and strange voices were heard when no one was there.

At Hawkins and Ransom Halls, cadets have reported that, during the night, they wake out of a sound sleep unable to move or scream and find it very difficult to breathe. At Sabine Field, the gate to the football field is often guarded by an unseen cadet. People have also reported the sound of ghostly footsteps.

## THE WHITE HOUSE

The spirit of Mrs. Martin Brown is said to haunt the historic White House Inn of Wilmington, Vermont. Both staff and guests have reported unexplainable cold spots, doors that open by themselves and visible apparitions. The inn itself has a vast attic with creaks included, a dungeon-like basement with dark areas and coal boilers, a locking iron vault and even a hidden staircase. The White House was built in 1915 as a private summer home for lumber baron Martin Brown.

One guest reported being visited in the middle of the night by an elderly lady who sat in a chair by the bed and said, "One Mrs. Brown in this room is quite enough!" It so happened that the guest and the original mistress of the house were both named Mrs. Brown.

## ENOSBURG FALLS OPERA HOUSE

Back in the early 1900s, "Willy," the son of a laborer, fell while working in the attic. He broke his leg and died there, forgotten by everyone. This good-humored ghost likes to steal playbooks and move props. He hasn't been seen, but many have reported hearing ghostly footsteps in the attic.

## THE UNDERGROUND RAILROAD

Vermont has a long history of opposition to slavery. Many Vermonters opposed slavery and helped runaway slaves throughout the pre–Civil War period. In 1777, Vermont's constitution became the first in the country to abolish slavery. While the federal Fugitive Slave Law of 1793 supported the "rights" of slave owners to reclaim their "property" in any state of the Union, many Vermonters secretly or openly resisted the law, and the legislature and the courts made it as difficult as possible for slave owners to remove escaped slaves from Vermont.

The underground railroad was especially active in Vermont from 1830 to 1860. Most of the fugitives who went to Canada through New England passed through Vermont, with the majority passing on the route from Brattleboro to Montpelier. While there are no clear records on the total number of fugitives to pass through Vermont, one underground railroad agent in Norwich, which was not one of the main routes, assisted six hundred escaped slaves.

## THE TOWER GHOST OF VERMONT COLLEGE

College Hall Chapel was built in the 1830s in Montpelier, Vermont. According to legend, in the late 1800s, a girl died in one of the towers. An autopsy of the young lady, who was murdered, revealed that the left side of her body went numb due to the fact that she had been shot behind her left ear.

Years later, a security guard was taking a group of students up to the tower when one of the girls complained that the left side of her body suddenly went numb. Other unexplained events include a pipe organ that sometimes plays on its own and ethereal breezes blowing within the building that occur seemingly out of nowhere as you walk along.

## "GOOD EVENING"

People who enjoy a nightly stroll beside an old graveyard in Cabot, Vermont, have reported being accompanied by a Mr. Anders, who passed away in the mid-1900s. Sometimes their stroll is silent, while at other times Mr. Anders tips his hat and bids them a friendly "good evening." According to historical documents, Mr. Anders was the caretaker of the cemetery until his death.

## HOW BARRE TOWN GOT ITS NAME

The story begins in 1788 when two pioneers—John Goldsbury and Samuel Rogers—and their families moved to Vermont from Massachusetts and trekked through the Green Mountain wilderness where land was cheap. Other pioneers followed in short order, coming from Massachusetts, Connecticut, Rhode Island and New Hampshire. They all settled in Wildersburgh, nearly twenty thousand acres of wilderness chartered to William Williams and sixty others in 1780. However, none of these people ever settled there. It took Goldsbury and Rogers to establish a community.

At the present West Hill Farm in Barre Town, you will find on one of the buildings a sign bearing this inscription: "At a town meeting held at this site September 3, 1793 occurred a fight between Jonathan Sherman of Barre, Mass., and Capt. Thompson of Holden, Mass., for the privilege of naming the town. Sherman won and named the town Barre."

Yet, there is another possibility. The townspeople, at a meeting in September 1793, decided to erect "a house of worship" and voted that the person contributing the most money for the building should have the right to name the town. Ezekiel Dodge Wheeler came through with the equivalent of $310 and promptly named the town Barre. But historian J.W. Ramsay refers to the fight and goes on with this eye-opening sentence: "This (the fight) is corroborated by the action of the town which, 12 years later, in September 1805, 'voted to destroy the note given by Mr. Wheeler and not collected,' thus carrying the impression that the note was never given a bona fide business transaction."

## AN UNEXPECTED FIND

The following is from the *Vermont Phoenix* on May 27, 1887: "Something of a sensation was occasioned last Monday by a report that the workmen engaged in excavating the cellar for W.G. Doolittle's house on High street had unearthed a human skeleton. The report proved true, and hundreds of people visited the spot

during the day to view the remains and conjecture over the mystery surrounding them. Several of the village doctors made a partial examination of the skeleton, which was in a good state of preservation, but found themselves unable to impart any further information than that the skeleton had been in the ground a good many years, and was that of a man of Anglo-Saxon race about six feet in height and under rather than beyond middle life. There were two small holes through the skull above the left ear, and a larger one back of the ear; but as none of these holes were round, and all were located upon the line of the sutures, it was impossible to regard them as certain evidences of foul play. No indications of a coffin or other surroundings were observed by the workmen, and nobody remembered when the spot was used for burial purposes. The most probable theory seemed to be, therefore, that, inasmuch as the premises were occupied some 25 years ago by Dr FJ Higginson, the skeleton was that of a 'subject' used by him or one of his students and afterward disposed of in the manner indicated. On Tuesday, however, a second skeleton was unearthed near the same spot, and on the following day a third one. In these latter cases the remains were much more decayed; but in the case of skeleton No. 2 a few old fashioned wrought iron nails and other indications were found. No. 3 was brought to light by the removal of a tree some 18 inches in diameter which grew above it. The skeletons were all within a few feet of each other and were about three feet under the surface.

"The finding of the remains of so many different individuals under such circumstances seems to be pretty strong evidence that the spot, which is on the brow of an elevated bluff, was used as a family burial plot by some former owner. Of our oldest inhabitants, however, none remember the time when it was used for this purpose; 'Uncle John' Putnam, the venerable keeper of the Hinsdale toll bridge, is very sure that he recollects being told by some previous old inhabitant that members of the Willard family were buried upon the spot in question. The Willards were ancestors of Miss Betsey Willard, who died only a few years ago, and of Asa Green, who was postmaster here for many years about the time of Jackson's administration. Green built the house adjacent to Mr. Doolittle's lot, since occupied by Dr Higginson, Dr OR Post and Mr. John Retting, the present occupant. If this explanation of the mystery is the true one, it goes to show one of the disadvantages of interment in a private cemetery with no stone or other memorial to mark the spot."

## CAPTAIN MOREY'S MOONLIGHT HAUNTING

History tells us that the steam engine was invented by Robert Fulton. However, it was actually invented by a man named Samuel Morey. In 1793, he fitted a paddle wheel and steam engine to a small boat and powered up and down the Connecticut River. Legend has it that this was done on a Sunday morning, when the town was at church, so as to avoid ridicule if he failed. Credit for the first successful steamboat line goes to Robert Fulton and his financier, Chancellor Robert Livingston. This was a cause for contention, as Morey claims that they took some of his ideas. Captain Morey was so angered that he sunk his boat, the *Aunt Sally*, to the bottom of Lake Morey (named in honor of Samuel Morey) in Fairlee, Vermont. On still, moonlit nights, the *Aunt Sally* rises to the lake's surface and floats without sound or ripple as the ghost of Captain Morey watches from shore.

## SHELBURNE MUSEUM'S HAUNTED DUTTON HOUSE

The Dutton House was built in Cavendish, Vermont, in 1782. It was unoccupied for forty years and later donated and moved to the Shelburne Museum in 1950. It was disassembled and moved to Shelburne, where it was put back together piece by piece. It also came with at least one ghost. Many museum employees and volunteers will not work in the building alone. They report hearing slamming doors, footsteps and ghostly voices when they know that no one else is in the building. Some dare not step foot into the house at all. One employee reports that on her first day on the job as a tour guide, she went upstairs and noticed an older man with a white shirt and scruffy face hunkering down under the slope of the roof. Another museum tour guide mentioned that she has heard the sound of a little girl crying.

## HAUNTED STAGECOACH STOP

Averill Stand, now a Historic Site, was built in 1787 and was for many years the stagecoach stop between Bennington and Brattleboro on what is now Route 9. The Averill family managed the stagecoach stand on the site, hence the name Averill Stand, as well as the tavern and inn. The family cemetery is on a small plot of land adjacent to the old pasture and contains the bodies of many of the house's former occupants. One of those, Lavina Field Averill, is believed to have died in childbirth in the home, and it is thought that she may be the spirit who has, on several occasions, placed missing items on the kitchen counter. One visitor reports having seen a young woman in old clothing in the dining room. At night, always between 10:30 p.m. and 11:40 p.m., the current occupant's dogs run to the back door, barking, and watch someone or something cross the backyard and walk to the old driveway. Some unseen being repeatedly rings the doorbell on snowy nights, leaving no trace of human footsteps. Perhaps it is Lavina, or perhaps it's Mrs. Brown, the wife of former lumber baron Martin Brown, who lived in the home for many years in the early 1900s and died there. Mrs. Brown is known to visit at least one of the adjoining houses in which she also resided. The house is noted for the repeated observations of spirit-sensitive folks of the warmth, friendliness and welcoming feeling in the place, which many attribute to the spirits of the house.

## THE INFAMOUS EMILY'S BRIDGE OF STOWE

No one really knows the true story behind the Emily's Bridge legend. Ghostly activities have been reported by many over the years, but there is no proof that "Emily" really existed or that any of the following stories are true.

In the nineteenth century, a girl was going to elope with the man of her dreams, even though her parents disliked the man entirely. He told her to meet him at the covered bridge nearest to their homes at noon on the next day. When she got there, no one was there. She waited for hours, and he never showed. She was so desperate for his love that she committed suicide.

Supposedly, if you go there at night and drive your car, she will sometimes call out for "help" and scratch your vehicle or do something to it as you go through. Also, you might see a whitish glowing figure walk up and down the bridge.

Another version is that a woman died (probably by her own hands) and haunts "her" bridge. She died in the 1800s, and people (and cars and horses) have, from time to time, gotten scratches from unseen nails. Lights can be seen, and noises can also be heard.

## The Legend of Boots Berry

Any self-respecting Vermont inn has a resident ghost or two. The Green Mountain Inn located in Stowe is no exception. As a matter of fact, it has a very unique tap-dancing ghost.

The inn itself is more than 173 years old, and during that time, it has welcomed a variety of guests from famous celebrities to the rowdiest of individuals. The inn was also home to a local man named Boots Berry, whose life ended on the grounds of the historic inn.

Boots was the son of the inn's horseman and chambermaid. He was actually born at the inn—room 302—in 1840. During that time, the room was located on the third floor as part of the servants' quarters. He grew up in and around the building and took over his father's work there while Boots was in his twenties.

He became known as a respected horseman and caretaker of the inn's horses. He was also responsible for providing fresh horses for the daily stagecoach. On one particular morning, the stagecoach team bolted and began to run away with passengers onboard. Boots was quick to react and stopped the runaway stage, saving the lives of the passengers inside. He was awarded a medal for heroism, and he became well known and popular throughout the county.

Unfortunately, his newfound popularity also led to his downfall. He became unreliable and took to drinking and to women, perhaps to an excessive amount of both. He eventually lost his job at the inn. After that, he traveled the country and wound up in a New Orleans jail, where he learned to tap dance from a fellow prisoner.

At the beginning of 1902, Boots found his way back to Stowe. He was broke and only carried the tattered clothes on his back. Shortly after he arrived, there was a severe snowstorm that trapped a little girl on the roof of the inn. Boots found his way to the roof and lowered the little girl to safety. Just when she was safe on the ground, Boots lost his footing on the ice-covered roof and fell to his death. The roof he was on was directly above room 302, where he was born. On stormy days, it is said that you can hear Boots Berry tap dancing on the roof.

## Theatrical Spirits

People working at or visiting St. Alban's Welden Movie Theater (which used to be a jail during the past century) have experienced several strange and unexplained encounters. The projection booths have been a spot of unusual activity. Movies have started by themselves, and voices can be heard in the old booths. The basement, which still has the remains of old jail cells, gives one the feeling of being watched. An old man with a white sweater has been seen walking around the basement. He is supposedly an elderly homeless man who took up residence there years ago. Apparently, he passed away but has never left the building.

The basement door also has been known to fly open even when latched.

## The Sleeping Sentinel

"The Sleeping Sentinel" of Groton, Vermont, is the most notable private of the Civil War. Historians and writers of that period, and ever since, have written many words about the remarkable Groton soldier—Private William Scott.

Private Scott had been court-martialed, and he was sentenced to be put to death by a firing squad on September 9, 1861. He had been found guilty of falling asleep at his post while on watch on the Potomac, where he had been assigned to guard the Chain Bridge and, thus, the nation's capital. Scott was found asleep there on August 31, 1861, between the hours of 3:00 a.m. and 4:00 a.m.

According to the Articles of War at that time, General Orders required that a sentry found asleep on duty should be shot. Four days before the Vermont regiment started the guarding of this strategic bridge, the Union forces had been badly beaten at Manassas Junction. General P.G.T. Beauregard's Confederate army was about ten miles away, south of the river, and a sentinel asleep at his post could have helped cause the fall of Washington. All accounts written about the Sleeping Sentinel report that Private Scott had actually volunteered to take the place of a sick comrade and was serving his second consecutive night of sentry duty when he was found asleep by the officer of the guard. He was immediately arrested.

Conflicting reports indicate that officers and enlisted men appealed to Brigadier General Smith, through a signed petition bearing 191 signatures, asking for a pardon. The chaplain, the Reverend Moses P. Parmalee, is believed to have presented to President Lincoln late Sunday evening the execution planned for Monday morning. Another story actually tells of Lincoln sending the pardoning order and then, worried about the situation, ordering his carriage to drive the ten miles to make certain that Scott's life was spared.

One conclusive piece of evidence was a letter revealed in a book written in 1936 entitled *Abraham Lincoln and the Sleeping Sentinel of Vermont*. The book explains that General McClellan wrote to his wife on September 8, 1861, the evening before the execution was to have taken place. He wrote, "Mr. Lincoln came this morning to ask me to pardon a man that I had ordered to be shot."

Several months after the pardon, on April 16, 1862, William Scott was sent with a contingency of 192 men to destroy the Confederate rifle pits across the Warwick River at Lee's Mills, Virginia. Only about 100 men returned from that mission. Private Scott fell mortally wounded while struggling up a riverbank with a wounded soldier on his shoulders. He is known to have saved several men from drowning in the muddy waters of that river.

## DEVIL CATS

Some call them devil cats while others call them beauties of nature. Vermont history is full of accounts regarding mountain lions prowling the woods of Vermont. Supposedly, the last catamount was shot in the town of Barnard in 1981; the species was all but exterminated by the end of the nineteenth century.

Yet, catamount sightings persist every year, with the first recorded sighting near Craftsbury, Vermont, in 1942. Since 1990, sightings have increased even more. Some believe that the State of Vermont knows of the catamount's existence, and there is a conspiracy or a coverup. According to the Vermont Department of Wildlife, there is no evidence supporting the existence of the legendary cat in the green mountains of Vermont.

## OLD BARLOW STREET SCHOOL

This old schoolhouse was built before the turn of the century. It was also used in the St. Albans Haunted House Halloween Event from 1979 to 1989. During the 1920s, a janitor died from a heart attack in a girl's restroom that was located in the cellar. Cold spots and odd sensations have occurred here, as well as an apparition appearing in a window in the south wing upstairs. The particular window refuses to remain closed after attempts to nail it shut. Sounds of footsteps have also been heard in that location as well as lights going off and on. People have reported hearing eerie voices.

## THE MOURNING STATUE

The Bowman House is located right across the street from the Bowman Mausoleum in the Cuttingsville Cemetery. Made wealthy from his tanning business, Mr. John P. Bowman built a mausoleum to hold the remains of his wife and children; the site includes a life-size statue of him, flowers in hand, walking up the steps in grief. If you drive along Route 103 in Cuttingsville, the eerie site of a ghostly white figure standing outside the door of the

Laurel Glen Mausoleum with a wreath and key in one hand and a top hat in the other may startle you. Yet it is merely a statue of Mr. Bowman, who, along with his family, is interred within the walls of the great stone vault.

The life-size statue of Mr. Bowman has been visible at the steps of the mausoleum since 1881, when the wealthy farmer had the vault constructed to house his wife and two daughters. Inside the crypt is a life-size statue of his oldest daughter, who died when she was an infant, along with busts of his wife and his other daughter, who tragically died within seven months of each other. Ten years later, in 1891, Mr. Bowman passed away and was also buried within the crypt.

Although strange occurrences have been reported around the mausoleum at night, the house across the street from the cemetery seems to be the hotspot for ghostly haunts. Some believe that the ghosts of Bowman and his family still reside within the mansion they once occupied during life. The mansion stood vacant for years but was eventually purchased. The new owners have reported seeing spirits of the Bowman family throughout the house. As a matter of fact, it is so haunted that the owners will no longer stay at the house after dark.

## HIDDEN TREASURE

Over the years, many treasure hunters have descended on Malletts Bay in Colchester, Vermont, in search of a legendary bounty within the sunken ship *Horatio Gates*. The ship was a nineteenth-century vessel reportedly carrying $50,000 in British gold. Needless to say, no one has yet found the treasure, and although history indicates that there really was such a ship, the legendary treasure could just be a myth. Worse yet, any treasure found on state property would belong to the State of Vermont. A 1987 law establishes that all shipwrecks on the Vermont side of Lake Champlain and anything on those ships are considered a public resource and thus all belong to the people of the state of Vermont. If there really is a treasure, maybe it's better off staying hidden.

## JONATHAN WHEELOCK'S HAUNTED FARMHOUSE

The home was a farmhouse in Cavendish, Vermont, built by Deacon Jonathan Wheelock in 1789, when he founded the first Episcopalian church there. Wheelock was the victim of a violent accident that took his life. Encounters of classic poltergeist activity have been reported within the house. Examples include things not being where they were left, items moved from room to room when no one else was in the house, objects falling off of shelves and so forth. On rare occasions, witnesses would wake up and see a bluish form, vaguely human-shaped, either gazing at them or out the window of the rooms. Reports vary based on eyewitness accounts of the ghostly sightings.

## THE EDDY BROTHERS

The Eddy brothers, William and Horatio, lived on a farm and were considered the "psychic mediums" of Chittenden, a small hamlet near Rutland, Vermont. Spiritualists began calling Chittenden the "Spirit Capital of the Universe." In 1874, the *New York Daily Graphic* assigned Henry Olcott to investigate the rumors of strange happenings in the house of the Eddy family. After ten weeks in the Vermont home, Olcott, who had had no previous psychic experiences, came away with a dislike of his gruff hosts and a remarkable story, which he told in fifteen articles.

During ten weeks of investigation, Olcott claimed that he saw about four hundred apparitions of all sizes, sexes and races issue from their cabinet. The chief apparitions were a giant American Indian named Santum and an American Indian woman by the name of Honto. Olcott had every facility for investigation—he measured the height and weight of the apparitions, roamed freely about and became quite satisfied that the explanation of impersonation was insufficient. He found that the production of materialized forms was William Eddy's specialty. Horatio Eddy usually sat before a cloth screen, not a cabinet, and, unlike his brother, was always in sight. Musical instruments were played behind the screen, and phantom hands showed themselves over the edge. If the same séance was held in darkness, the phenomena became very powerful. Vigorous American Indian dances shook the floor, and the room resounded with yells and whoops. "As an exhibition of pure brute force," Olcott writes in one of the articles, "this Indian dance is probably unsurpassed in the annals of such manifestation."

## THE BROOKFIELD FLOATING BRIDGE

Brookfield is located just south of Williamstown, in Orange County, Vermont. It is the site of the famous Floating Bridge, buoyed by 380 barrels—the only floating bridge in Vermont. The three-hundred-foot bridge spans Sunset Lake, which is too deep to support a pillared structure. In 1820, the bridge was made up of floating logs, but the logs had to be replaced each year. Tarred barrels then became the solution for a number of years until modern times, when they were replaced by plastic barrels filled with Styrofoam.

It is an eerie sensation driving across a bridge that floats on water but it's an experience you won't soon forget.

## WHEN BARNS FLY

Shelburne Museum's round barn greets visitors the moment they arrive. Most people have no idea that the enormous, round barn was actually moved there by helicopter in 1985 and 1986. It was built in 1901 by Fred "Silo" Quimby, over eighty miles away from Shelburne, in Passumpsic, Vermont. The three-story barn is sixty feet tall and eighty feet in diameter. Imagine the sight of such a huge structure carried by a Skycrane helicopter over the hills and valleys of Vermont.

However, the story is not entirely true, despite the fact that many people believe and will stubbornly attest to the fact that they did indeed see a barn flying over the Green

Mountains of Vermont. What they actually saw was just the barn's silo, which was the round core of the barn. A remarkable feat in itself but not nearly as grandiose as some believe!

## A GHOST IN EVERY BUILDING?

Two hundred yards away from Castleton State College is an abandoned building. The interior is filled with untouched museum pieces that appear to have been left behind. Although there is no way to enter the building, the objects inside seem to move and get tossed about on their own.

Within the walls of a dorm, an apparition of a student wearing an orange T-shirt and jeans awakens people in the middle of the night. Apparently, he hanged himself and is still hanging around. Also, Ellis Hall has been part of Castleton State College for years. On the second floor of this building, a female student killed herself. Students hear her flushing toilets and running the showers and the sink in the bathroom. Almost every building at Castleton State is reputed to be haunted.

## The "Other" Vermont Teddy Bear

When people think of Vermont and teddy bears, the following isn't quite what comes to mind. Here is the story of another, lesser-known Vermont teddy bear with a bit more infamous past.

Clarence Adams was a man of diverse skills. He was the Vermont state representative, selectman for the town of Chester, church deacon, incorporator of the Chester Savings Bank and a convicted criminal who burglarized the town of Chester for nearly sixteen years. He robbed by night, stealing from every store on Main Street at least once and from some as many as six times. His first victims were close family members and friends, and then he moved on to neighbors. Although this upstanding citizen was the one who terrorized this town, he was the first to help his victims with plans to capture the thief. He sympathized with their losses, even going as far as to offer money from his own pocket for the reward for his own capture.

After many years of conning the town, Adams's burglary spree ended on the night of July 29, 1902. He robbed Waterman's Mill, unaware that Charles Waterman had rigged the window with a shotgun so that it would shoot the thief. Clarence Adams was convicted and sentenced to ten years in prison.

Adams wasn't finished tricking the town yet. After his first two years in prison, the *Vermont Journal* published the obituary of Clarence Adams. The town assumed that he was dead until a salesman in town returned from a business trip claiming to have encountered Adams at the Windsor Hotel in Montreal. Many others had also stepped forward with their stories of seeing Adams in their travels through Canada. No one really knows whether the town's famous burglar died in prison or faked his death and escaped to Canada.

In 2002, the people of Chester gave tribute to the capture and conviction of their "gentleman burglar" by creating their own 100th anniversary, limited-edition Clarence Adams teddy bear.

## COUNTRY CLUB GHOSTS

At the nearby Brattleboro Country Club on Dummerston Road, workers describe hearing garbled voices above the dining area of the country club. None of the waitresses like to close the dining area alone. Footsteps have been heard walking overhead, along with other various sounds. No one claims to know who the ghost or ghosts are.

## GREEN MOUNTAIN GOLD RUSH

After the California gold rush of 1849, whoever didn't make it straggled back to their respective states and countries to return to their former lives. One such gold seeker came home to Vermont about 1850 and went fishing at Buffalo Creek in Plymouth. As he cast his line, he couldn't help but think about the rush; looking down into the stream, he recognized a familiar glint in the water. He promptly grabbed a half-ounce nugget from the stream. That was the beginning of Vermont's own gold rush. The Rooks Mine was soon established nearby. Rooks was a stamp mill, where ore was crushed, and it leached the gold through a process involving acid and mercury, a practice that was long ago retired.

In the end, twenty-two thousand ounces of gold were taken from the mine at the top of the mountain. Fine gold and small nuggets can still be found in the stream, and probably in just about any other stream in Vermont. The Vermont gold rush continues to this day. Recreational gold prospecting is the fastest-growing family-oriented hobby in the nation today. Green Mountain Prospectors of Vermont boasts at least 515 members as of 2007.

## THE GREAT DISAPPOINTMENT

Atheist William Miller decided to found a religion of his own. Obsessed with death and the Judgment Day, Miller became convinced that Christ's Second Coming was revealed in biblical prophecy. In September 1822, Miller formally stated his conclusions in a twenty-point document: "I believe that the second coming of Jesus Christ is near, even at the door, even within twenty-one years—on or before 1843." The actual date that the world would come to an end was predicted to occur on October 22, 1844.

From 1840 onward, he transformed his personal beliefs into a national campaign. His followers, one of whom was a Vermont farmer, became known as "Millerites." This farmer had a seamstress make "ascension robes" for six of his best cows in preparation of Judgment Day. The farmer reasoned that on that final day "they [the cows] will come in mighty handy up there. It's a long trip and the kids will be wanting some milk."

The sun rose on the morning of October 23, 1844. Both Millerite leaders and followers were left generally bewildered and disillusioned. The world was still the same, and the Vermont farmer's cows were all dressed up with no place to go.

## EMILY LINGERS AT MARLBORO COLLEGE

A ghost named Emily lingers on in the distinctive Marlboro College. A century ago, Emily Mather and her mysterious lover came to an end not unlike the story of Romeo and Juliet. Sometime in the late nineteenth century, back when the college was a working farm, Emily fell in love with a traveling salesman who called on families within nearby Vermont villages. Her parents were very strict and forbade the relationship, ordering the young man away from their daughter. Devastated by the turn of events, the despondent salesman threw himself into a stream and drowned. Upon hearing the news, Emily climbed to the attic of her family's home and hanged herself. The home where Emily is said to have died is now known as Mather House, the college's main administration building. The stream where the heartbroken salesman drowned still flows through the college campus.

Suicide at the time was considered shameful and embarrassing for a family to endure. Emily was buried in an unmarked grave below her parents' barn, which was later remodeled into Dalrymple Hall, a building containing classrooms. Her body rested peacefully in the grave until the 1950s, when excavation to build the Howland House disinterred her anonymous burial site.

It is in the Howland House where unexplained occurrences have led some to believe that Emily's disturbed grave caused her spirit to walk among the living. Students have reported seeing a female figure wandering the campus at night, and many have felt uneasy when alone in Howland or Dalrymple during the evening hours. Cold spots and banging noises (with no apparent cause) are often encountered around the campus.

## THE YEAR WITHOUT A SUMMER

The year 1816 has gone down in the annals of New England history as "The Year There Was No Summer," the "Poverty Year" and "Eighteen Hundred and Froze to Death." The year began with a moderate but dry winter. Spring was late coming and continued to be very dry. The growing season from late spring to early fall suffered from a series of devastating cold waves that did major damage to the crops, greatly reducing the food supply. In areas of central and northern New England, the summer had only two extended periods without frost or near-freezing temperatures. A widespread snow fell in June. As a result, corn did not ripen and hay, fruits and vegetables were greatly reduced in quantity and quality.

The *North Star* of Danville, Vermont, reported in 1816: "June 5th was perhaps as warm and sultry a day as we have had since September—At night heat lightning was observed, but on Thursday morning the change of weather was so great that a fire was not only comfortable, but actually necessary. The wind during the whole day was as piercing and cold as it usually is the first of November and April. Snow and hail [ice pellets] began to fall about ten o'clock A.M., and the storm continued till evening, accompanied with a brisk wind, which rendered the habiliments of winter necessary for the comfort of those exposed to it…Probably no one living in the country ever witnessed such weather, especially of so long continuance."

July and August were equally cold and dismal. No one knows what may have caused such unusually cold and bleak weather throughout the entire year. Volcanic activity was mentioned as a possibility, as were sunspots, ocean temperatures, carbon dioxide and ozone issues, but nothing was conclusive. The final possible cause could have simply been a matter of chance, which is most likely what caused the weather (or lack thereof) in the summer of 1816.

## AN INN FULL OF GHOSTS

Quechee is an unusual name but a charming little town. The town and its spectacular Quechee Gorge are located next to what many consider to be the quintessential Vermont village: Woodstock. The Quechee Inn was built by Joseph Marsh IV in 1793. In 1845, the farm changed hands to John Porter and his wife, Jane. They lived there throughout the years and celebrated their fiftieth wedding anniversary in 1881. John passed away five years later, followed by Jane in 1900.

It is said that most of the supernatural activity at the twenty-four-room inn takes place between rooms 1 and 6. These are the rooms that long ago encompassed Jane Porter's parlor and her study. On one recent occasion, a former maintenance man was fixing the floor near room 3, which was supposed to be vacant, and heard odd noises. He sought out the innkeeper to ask if anyone was in room 3. She confirmed what she had told him earlier—that the room was vacant. The man was certain he had heard the door opening and closing and could hear footsteps. At another time, the innkeeper and the workman were up most of the night in a last-minute attempt to finish up some painting near the dining area. During the early morning hours, they both had a sensation of hair standing up on the back of their necks, and each felt like someone was watching them. Both of them then heard whistling in the area near the bar. The phone system also began to act strange, emitting a number of blinking lights. Slightly shaken by all that had occurred, the two continued their work and finished their task.

One day, a guest came down from her room one night suffering from a slight case of insomnia. As she walked across the main entry hallway to go into the common room to read, she saw a woman walking toward her from the dining room. When the guest looked that way again a second later, there was no one there. Her description to staff the next day matched that of Jane Porter. The staff at the inn believes that Mrs. Porter still walks the premises, checking on her house. In room 9, guests have reported hearing people walking overhead, which is just a storage area. A couple of guests mentioned that they heard footsteps just outside their door while someone or something was trying to turn the doorknob. They were the only guests in that area of the inn at that time. They also said that they could feel cold spots in the room. Other spirits are said to reside at the inn as well, including a boy thought to be Patrick Marsh. He plays tricks on people, hiding items and then returning them sometime later. He also is believed to be responsible for lights flickering or TVs going on and off.